It is definitely

no coincidence that

you happened to find this book!

It is certainly **not by chance** that you

opened it to this particular page. Some-

where in this life there's **a ✴ Miracle**

with your name on it, and

you are now about to

discover precisely

what it is!

♥ Inner Wisdom Publications

proudly presents additional...

Books

Get A Round Tuit 'N Do It™
How to Easily Transform **Procrastination** into ✳ **Accomplishment**!

My ✳ Miracle Manifestation Manual™
A Personal **31-Day** ✳ **Miracle Journal** for You

Everything You Ever Wanted to Know About The 15-Minute ✳ Miracle™

The 15-Minute ✳ Miracle  Playbook™
How to Create Your Own **Incredible Coincidences** on Purpose!

Gifts

✳ Miracle Attraction Chest™

(a magical chest full of inspiring books and delightful gifts)

(See pages 137-139 for book and product descriptions.)

The 15-Minute Miracle™

Revealed

Jacquelyn Aldana ✶ S.o.L.

(inspired by Ron Aldana)

♥ **Inner Wisdom Publications**

Los Gatos, California

Copyright © 1998 by Jacquelyn Aldana ✝ S.o.L.

Published by: ♥ *Inner Wisdom Publications*

Mailing Address: PO Box 1341 ✳ Los Gatos, CA 95031-1341, USA
Telephone: (408) 353-2050 ✳ 1-(888) In The Flow (1-888-468-4335)
Fax : (408) 353-4663 ✳ **E-Mail Address**: amiracle@ix.netcom.com
Web Site: http://www.15-MinuteMiracle.com

Logo by Kat Thomas
Edited by Laurie Masters and Pamela Tablak
Cover design and illustration by LaVon Coffin
Computer Graphics by Image Club via Corel Gallery
Inspiration and unconditional l♥ve provided by Ron Aldana

The contents of this book are a reflection of the author's experience and are in no way intended to take the place of professional medical treatment. The author does not dispense medical advice nor prescribe the use of any technique as a form of treatment for physical, mental, or emotional health challenges with or without the advice of a physician or healthcare professional.

Library of Congress Catalog Card Number 97-094033

Publisher's - Cataloging In Publication
(Provided by Quality Books, Inc.)

Aldana, Jacquelyn.
    The 15-minute miracle revealed / by Jacquelyn Aldana

    -- 1st ed.
    p. cm
    Fifteen-minute miracle
    Fifteen minute miracle
    Includes bibliographical references and index.
    ISBN 0-9656741-7-7

    1. Self-help techniques 2. Self-actualization (Psychology)
  3. Self-realization. I. Title. II. Title: Fifteen-minute miracle
  III. Title: Fifteen minute miracle
    BF632.A53 1998   158'.1
                            QB197-41202

If you are unable to order this book from your local bookseller, you may order directly from the publisher by calling **TOLL FREE 1-(888) 468-4335**

Printed in the United States of America - First Printing 1998
10 9 8 7 6 5 4 3 2 1 - 02 01 99 98

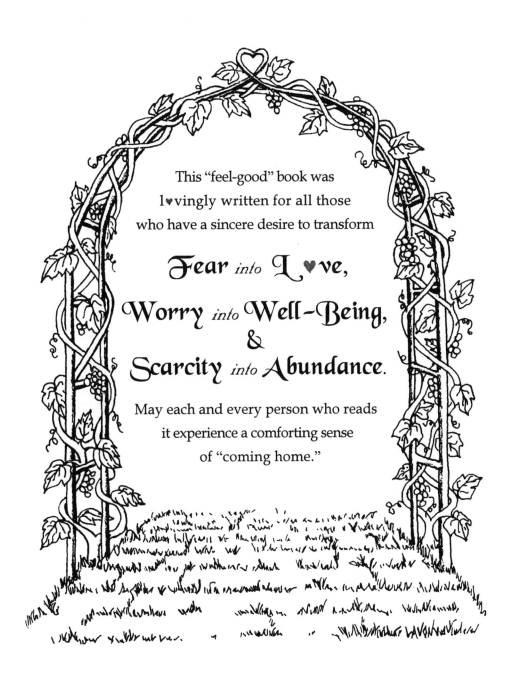

This "feel-good" book was
l♥vingly written for all those
who have a sincere desire to transform

Fear into L♥ve,

Worry into Well-Being,
&
Scarcity into Abundance.

May each and every person who reads
it experience a comforting sense
of "coming home."

Dedicated to ✦ My Best Friend

This book may never have been written had it not been for my l♥ving husband, Ron. He has truly been my dearest friend for the last quarter of a century. We met in 1973 and were married less than a year later. He faithfully promised that if I would marry him, he would take pleasure in "spoiling me rotten," and he certainly has lived up to his promise. Ron has been consistently positive, encouraging, and very supportive over the years, and I have always wanted to find a way to properly reciprocate.

When I asked him why he wanted to spend the rest of his life with me, he gently took both of my hands in his and gazed at me softly. He smiled warmly and said with an impish twinkle in his eye, "I l♥ve you just the way you are, plus I also see a promising *potential* within you!" In that moment, I had no idea what he was referring to, but he certainly made me feel special!

Well, my dear Ron, you had to wait a while, but I think my so-called "potential" finally emerged. When your doctors told you that you had only three months to live in 1991, I became absolutely *determined* to find a way to help you regain your wellness. After exhausting all known possibilities, I didn't know what else to do. For lack of a better idea **I simply asked for a ✦ Miracle**! That's when I realized that all things really *are* possible when we focus only upon answers and solutions! Although this near-fatal episode certainly challenged us both, it turned out to be the catalyst that allowed me to discover what we now l♥vingly refer to as our 15-Minute ✦ Miracle™.

It is because of you, my l♥ve, that so many others who are actively looking for answers and seeking solutions may be able to find them. Because of you, I was divinely inspired to write this book and share a message that has the potential to make a positive difference in countless lives. I always knew that you were very special. Thank you, my friend, for just being you.

Table of Contents

Introduction

Part 1

Part 2

Part 3

Part 4

Table of Contents

(continued)

Foreword

This book is about a simple process that is sure to become a *household word* on a global basis! It quickly enables each person who reads it to feel "on top of the world" almost immediately. It was created as a result of Jacquelyn Aldana's determination to find a way to help save her husband's life. Initially, it served to bring her *own* life back into balance. Then her husband, Ron, casually experimented with it and ultimately became **cancer free** (in spite of doctors insisting that he only had **three months to live)**!

As she shared her discovery with friends and family, they in turn shared it with *their* circle of acquaintances. Just by word of mouth, the intriguing little process known as The 15-Minute Miracle began to generate inquiries from hundreds of people all over the country. Due to popular demand, Ron and Jacquelyn finally agreed to offer playful workshops (playshops) for those who were eager to learn it.

The extraordinary results that ordinary people began to experience were nothing short of miraculous. Those who were physically challenged began to enjoy **better health**. Many who were financially limited suddenly began to enjoy **abundance and prosperity**. Several who had been struggling with relationship issues, began to relate to others with far greater **ease and harmony**. In short, everyone who experimented with this magical little process, found a way to enjoy a consistent sense of well-being. It seems to offer benefits for everyone who does it, and the results are often quite dramatic.

Jacquelyn wrote this book to clearly reveal the secrets of her success. She believes that it was divinely inspired and considers it a magnificent gift for all to enjoy. Because the principles are based upon universal laws, The 15-Minute Miracle transcends age, culture, religion, and limiting beliefs. It even works for those who are quite skeptical of ideas that suggest that you can have a happy and prosperous life without struggling and sacrificing. It is intended to enable you to feel good about life, no matter what challenges you may be facing. It shows you how it's possible to *deliberately* transform your fondest dreams into physical realities with incredible ease.

What Jacquelyn discovered along her enlightening journey is what *you* can expect to experience for yourself as you read this thought-provoking book. With heartfelt appreciation and enormous enthusiasm, she explains how absolutely *anyone* can attract Miracles and extraordinary coincidences into their lives on a consistent and predictable basis.

The 15-Minute ✳ Miracle™ Revealed offers a perfect balance of familiar concepts combined with fresh and creative ideas. It can't help but ignite your enthusiasm! Once you see how quickly and easily it works for you, you will be eager to share it with those near and dear to you. In my opinion, this empowering book has the potential to uplift the consciousness of the entire planet! Find out how *you* can harness the element of synchronicity, and become the master of your own destiny. Discover how you can actually *choose* what happens to you in life by setting aside just **15 minutes a day** for yourself. You, too, can experience a whole new way of life that invites your desires to be realized and your dreams to come true.

Harold McCoy, Director and Founder
Ozark Research Institute—Fayetteville, Arkansas

✴ Acknowledgment

I wish to acknowledge all the wise and wonderful teachers who came before me to show me the way. I want to particularly thank my positive role model, Oprah Winfrey, and my gentle mentors, Louise Hay, Dr. Wayne Dyer, Dr. Deepak Chopra, and Neale Donald Walsch. I am especially grateful to Jerry and Esther Hicks, who consistently encouraged me to focus upon the path of unlimited positive possibilities through their inspiring audiotapes. All of you were the wind beneath my wings when I was learning to fly. Thank you for being the shining lights who made such a pleasant and empowering difference in my life!

As I eagerly searched for enlightenment, I was greatly influenced by a multitude of inspiring books and thought-provoking audio and videotapes. The ones that uplifted me the most are listed in the bibliography as…

✴Inspirational Food for Thought.

Most of all, I want to offer my warmest thanks to You, ✴God, for You are the unconditionally l♥ving Power in my life who gently guided and supported me every step of the way. I so appreciate Your comforting presence and Your infinite patience. Thank You for always providing abundant enlightenment as we make our way in the world. Please continue to remind us of who we *really* are on a spiritual level—divine extensions of Your pure, positive life-force energy. I am so grateful that You blessed us with the magnificent gift of *free will,* and I am especially pleased that You gave each of us the fertile seeds of unlimited potential to sing the song that we came here to sing!

Jacquelyn Aldana ✴S.o.L.
✴Student Of Life ✴Spirit Of Light
✴Sender Of L♥ve ✴So Obviously Lucky

You're ✳ **Great** and I'm ✳ **Grateful!**

If this book "touches your heart" and makes a positive difference in your life, please give credit to the remarkable people below who provided the l♥ve, support, and resources that enabled me to write it. I wish to express my heartfelt appreciation to…

- Ron Aldana for being my husband, my best friend, and my most avid supporter.
- Heathcliff Aldana for his l♥ve, playful demeanor, and extraordinary enthusiasm!
- Ronnie and Kim Aldana for their valuable feedback and perpetual encouragement.
- Jonathan Bachelor for always being a magnificent shining light for me to emulate.
- Gayle Bradshaw for reminding me to keep "The ✳ Miracle Message" purely positive!
- Trace and Debi Butkovich for training my computer to be more "author friendly!"
- LaVon Coffin for the incredibly beautiful book cover she created for this book.
- Stephanie Coffin for proving it's truly possible to transcend an "incurable" dis-ease.
- John and Elinor Crittenden for giving me the precious and divine gift of life.
- Carol Gibbons for persistently sharing "The ✳ Miracle" with everyone on the planet!
- Sunnee Kee for the countless hours she worked to enable me to write this book.
- Larry LeVine for his impeccable integrity, generosity, and innate visionary talent.
- Al Loukinen for being the only dad I ever knew. I am all that I am because of him.
- Elsie (Duffie) Loukinen for taking me in to raise me as her own. Thanks, Mom!
- Laurie Masters, (my *Precision Revision Angel*) for her extraordinary editing talents.
- Pamela Masters for pouring forth her endless inspiration, love, and magnificent self.
- Harold and Gladys McCoy for endorsing this work and inviting me to speak at ORI.
- Detta Penna for the time she took out of her busy life to be my gentle mentor.
- Brooke Peterson for proving how this process easily creates unlimited abundance.
- Dan Poynter for teaching me how to self-publish my books with amazing ease!
- Pamela Tablak for her l♥ving support, editing talents, and computer teaching skills.
- Jodi Taylor for her loyalty and always being here to make my life so much easier.
- Kat Thomas for creating the beautiful "North Star Logo" that lights up my life.
- Dodie Veres for "bugging" me every day to offer seminars until I finally did it!
- John Van Drie for the amazing and magical healings he continues to provide.
- Leigh Wunce for giving me homework that led to the discovery of this process.
- Each and every person who in any way contributed to the creation of this book.

Disclaimer

What you are about

to read may cause you

to experience an extraordinary

sense of upliftment, self-empowerment,

and inexplicable joy. This book tends to be

physically, mentally, emotionally, and spiritually

addictive. The positive effects are extremely *contagious*

and may cause epidemic proportions of positive possibilities

with all those who come in direct contact with it! Should you

experience an overabundance of ✴ Miracles while applying

the simple principles, please set this book aside until

the euphoria subsides.

Warning

Under no circumstances should anyone ever indulge in

𝕿𝖍𝖊 15-𝕸𝖎𝖓𝖚𝖙𝖊 ✴ 𝕸𝖎𝖗𝖆𝖈𝖑𝖊 for more than 24 hours a day!

Please Read at Your Own Risk!

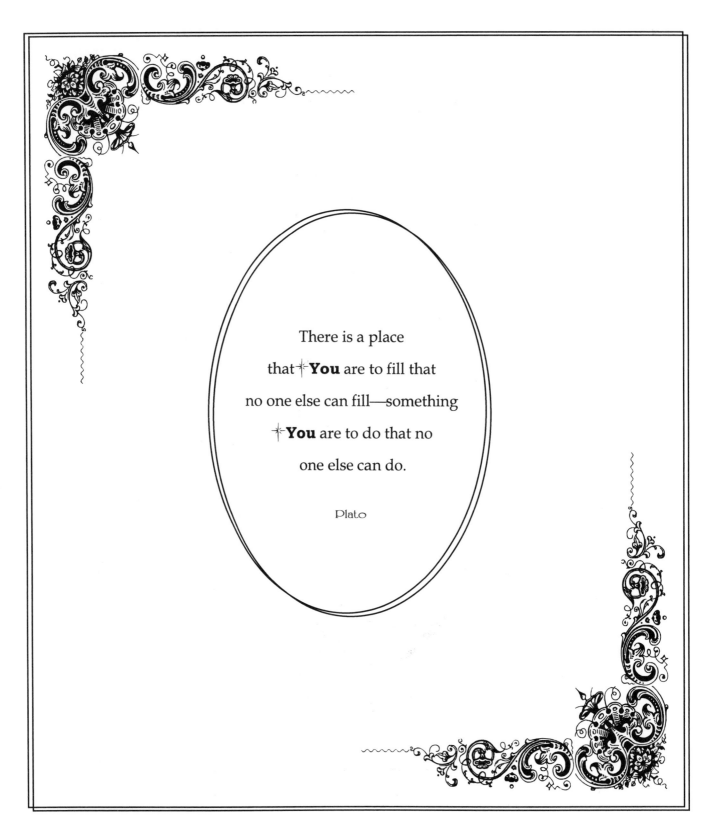

There is a place

that ✦**You** are to fill that

no one else can fill—something

✦**You** are to do that no

one else can do.

Plato

Introduction

- Shortcuts to Miracles

- From Stumbling Blocks to Stepping Stones

✳ Shortcut

…a simple way of doing
something more directly and
quickly than by ordinary means.
The 15-Minute ✳ Miracle provides an
easy-to-follow **ROAD MAP** that clearly
shows many intriguing and time-
saving *shortcuts* to ✳ Miracles!

Shortcuts to Miracles

There is an extremely quick and simple way for you to enjoy a delightfully positive difference in your life! This book tells you how you can accomplish this almost immediately, *regardless* of any challenges you may be experiencing at this time. Get comfortable, and give yourself permission to claim the next couple of hours exclusively for *you*. Enjoy discovering how you can *deliberately* attract Miracles and easily create "incredible coincidences" in your life in only **15 minutes a day**.

Because it is under 160 pages, and there is plenty of white space, you can read this entire book in approximately two to three hours. I have deliberately used **several different type styles** to emphasize that which is most important for you to comprehend. Although this tends to slow down your reading a bit, it actually results in a very positive benefit for *you*. It enables you to magically absorb and digest the empowering essence of *The 15-Minute Miracle*, so you can relax, have fun, and begin to experience more joy in life.

Although the wisdom expressed within the pages of this book was no doubt spiritually inspired, it is by no means meant to be religious in nature. Each person's religious and spiritual convictions are very personal, and I respectfully honor all paths that lead to Truth. You are invited to take what you can use, and simply leave the rest. The main objective is that you thoroughly enjoy yourself and...

*just have **fun** with it!*

✴ Stepping Stones

The greatest opportunities
(stepping stones) are often created
out of the biggest adversities (stumbling
blocks). Major challenges cause some people
to *break*, while they inspire others
to actually *break records!*

From Stumbling Blocks to ✳ Stepping Stones

Do you ever feel as though you are trying to swim upstream in the rivers of life? Do you feel like you're trying to walk through walls of resistance, instead of simply opening the doors of opportunity? Does it feel as though you have been trying to run through wet cement as you rush to meet the demands of the day? If so, you'll be glad to know that…

- You are certainly **not alone**!
- There is a much **easier way** to proceed.
- You can actually **choose** what happens to you in life!

Just prior to discovering The 15-Minute ✳ Miracle and writing this book, I was definitely at an all-time low in my own life. My husband, Ron, was suffering from a virulent cancer and was struggling to merely stay alive. Totally worn out from resisting life's challenges, we were both trying to find a way to simply get through just o-n-e m-o-r-e day.

Being Ron's full-time caregiver for well over two years began to take its toll on me. I was looking forward to a major "change" in my life, and I got exactly what I asked for. The next thing I knew, I was involuntarily launched into the so-called "change of life" (menopause)! Between extreme fatigue, power surges (commonly known as hot flashes), and unpredictable mood swings, everything seemed pretty overwhelming to me. In light of this arduous situation, Ron and I began to suffer a serious deterioration of the l♥ving relationship that we had shared for over twenty years. Life, as we knew it, was just not fun any more.

Whenever I feel extremely overwhelmed, I find it useful to stop everything and take time to write down what's bothering me. This enables me to more easily sort out what I need to do. One afternoon (after feeling as though I had run a twenty-six mile marathon with my feet tied together), I literally collapsed into my desk chair and scribbled out the following question:

"What exactly is my **purpose** *for even being here?"*

For some reason, I felt inexplicably *compelled* to write down the curious response that came into my mind. It was so strong that I couldn't possibly ignore it! As though an unseen hand was gently guiding my pen, I found myself writing the following statement:

*"***Discover** *the* ✦ **Truth,** *and* **share** *it with others."*

When I read it back, I was absolutely awestruck! It seemed so profound, yet I really didn't understand it—"What Truth?" I wondered. "What others?" The more I thought about it, the more I was convinced that I was losing my grip on reality. Out of the frustration of it all, I simply returned to my world of struggling to get through just o-n-e m-o-r-e day.

I was sure that I had set aside this issue, yet everything I picked up to read seemed to have the word "Truth" leaping off the page. The Truth being referred to was no ordinary truth. It was the **Big Truth**—the Truth about ✦ Life! It was uncanny how many times that word came up in everyday conversations. I began to wonder if it had suddenly become the universal word of choice. About one week after asking ✦ God to clarify my life's purpose, I came across the paper I had written it upon. When I reread the words, "Discover the ✦ Truth, and share it with others," my body became flooded with thrill bumps. **W-o-w!** I finally decided that this was not to be taken lightly!

What happened only a few hours later is truly a remarkable story. Out of my determination to find solutions, I honestly believe I was divinely led to discover the magical process that Ron and I now l♥vingly refer to as 𝕿𝖍𝖊 15-𝕸𝖎𝖓𝖚𝖙𝖊 ✦ 𝕸𝖎𝖗𝖆𝖈𝖑𝖊. The results of this discovery have surely been nothing short of miraculous. For openers, my less-than-perfect relationship with Ron was completely healed only twelve hours after applying the simple principles. Shortly after Ron began to do it, his health improved dramatically, and today he is totally **happy, healthy, and cancer-free!** When we began to share it with our friends and family, we noticed that they also experienced awesome results. After a while, so many people were calling on the phone and coming to the door for information that Ron and I had to offer organized gatherings to accommodate all of them.

The 15-Minute ✴ Miracle
literally took on a life of its own!

Shortly after the manuscript of this book had been reviewed by friends, relatives, and a few literary professionals, we began receiving advance orders from all over the United States and Canada. I was amazed that so many people had heard about it just by *word of mouth*. Several doctors and other healthcare professionals were convinced that The 15-Minute ✴ Miracle had positive value for their patients, while others just wanted the book for themselves or as a gift for their friends and l♥ved ones.

Ron and I feel so blessed to be able to share this empowering message with those who desire to hear it. At first, you may think this book is all about us, but as it turns out, it's really **all about you.** It reveals how you can deliberately attract whatever you consciously *choose* to experience in life. There really *is* an easier and more enjoyable way to play this ✴ Magnificent Game of Life, and I am eager to help you discover it for yourself! If you appreciate benefits such as…

✴Good **Health** ✴Abundant **Energy** ✴Unexpected **Income,**
✴L♥ving **Relationships** ✴A Sense of **Well-Being** ✴Delightful **Surprises,**

I think you will be absolutely thrilled with this intriguing and life-enhancing process called The 15-Minute ✴ Miracle. In fact, I'm sure you are going to enjoy it!

Laughter is the

Shortest Distance

between two people!

Victor Borge

Part 1

- How Every Day Can Be a ✴ Great Day!
- ✴ Answers to Your Questions

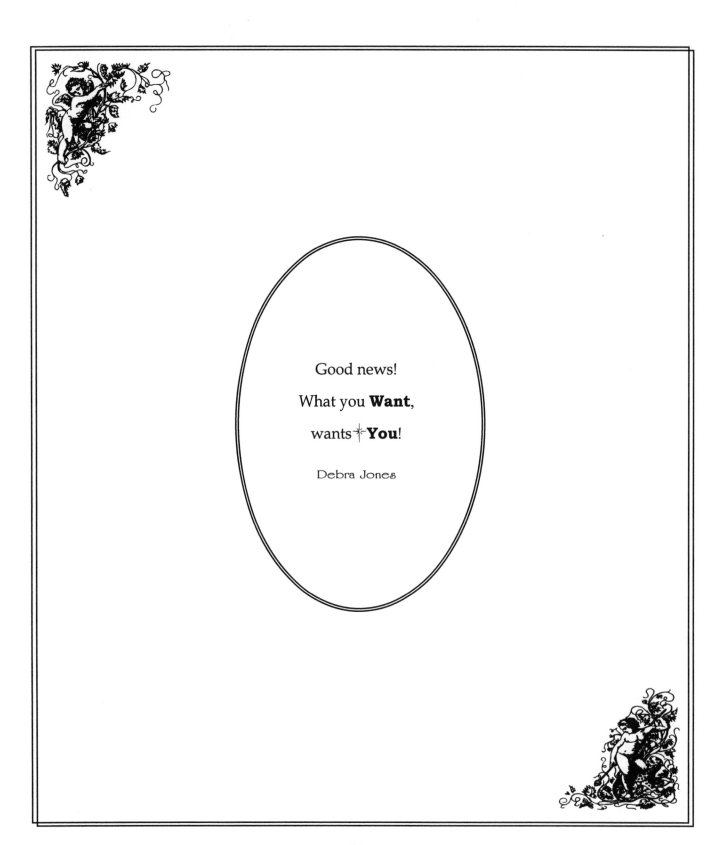

Good news!

What you **Want**,

wants **You**!

Debra Jones

How **Every Day** Can Be a **Great Day!**

Have you ever had one of those days that was so magical that you wished it would never end…you know, one of those days when it didn't matter what you did or how you did it, everything just naturally fell into place? Wouldn't it be wonderful if only there were a way to experience days like these on demand? Just imagine how glorious that would be! What usually happens, however, is that we go through life thinking we have no control over such things—that some days are just better than others. Right? **WRONG!**

You'll be glad to know that you can actually summon these miraculous days whenever you choose! This book promises to show you a simple way to access a magical process, which will enable you to create one good day after another. In fact, you will be able to experience *anything* you desire by merely applying a few simple principles. All you have to do is understand how certain universal laws work, so you can *allow* them to work in your favor. Yes, I know this all sounds too good to be true, so please don't take *my* word for it. Just follow the instructions in this book and see what happens! Don't be too surprised, however, if you start "soaring with eagles and flying with angels!"

The next few pages consist of the most frequently asked questions related to The 15-Minute Miracle. The answers will give you a better idea of what it's all about. Discover how you can consciously *choose* your life experiences. Learn how *every* day can be a *positive* day, and how you can easily attract and create whatever you really want in life *on purpose*. Prepare for an adventure that will very likely sweep you right off your feet! Get ready to **fall in l♥ve**—in l♥ve with Life and everything in it (including yourself)! Life absolutely adores you and is eager to offer you everything your heart desires. All *you* have to do is figure out what truly makes you happy—the rest is relatively easy!

11

Every question has an ✴**Answer**,

and every problem has a ✴**Solution**,

and all of the answers and solutions are ✴**Within**!

Jacquelyn Aldana ✴**S.o.L.**

Answers to Your Questions

1. ***What exactly is The 15-Minute✦Miracle?***

   It is probably one of the easiest and most delightful methods of attracting what you really want in life *on purpose!* This extremely simple process is fondly referred to as 𝕮𝔥𝔢 15-𝔐𝔦𝔫𝔲𝔱𝔢✦𝔐𝔦𝔯𝔞𝔠𝔩𝔢, because…

   - you can do it in **only 15 minutes a day**, anywhere, any time.
   - it offers a positive outcome to absolutely **anyone** who does it,
   - and the results are often so dramatic and life-changing that most people can only describe them as✦**Miracles**!

2. ***What benefits can I expect to derive from this process?***

   You are likely to experience an extraordinary sense of well-being right away! You may feel quite inspired, because it shifts your attention from the way you perceive things "to be" to the way things "could be" if all things were ideal. You will begin to see that there are many more possibilities than you may have realized! In short, 𝕮𝔥𝔢 15-𝔐𝔦𝔫𝔲𝔱𝔢✦𝔐𝔦𝔯𝔞𝔠𝔩𝔢 is designed to offer you the greatest number of benefits, in the shortest period of time, with the least amount of effort! The positive results that are available for you to enjoy are virtually limitless.

3. ***Can you give me some examples of what it has done for others?***

   𝕮𝔥𝔢 15-𝔐𝔦𝔫𝔲𝔱𝔢✦𝔐𝔦𝔯𝔞𝔠𝔩𝔢 has touched many lives in a variety of wonderful ways. Alice Cabral, who urgently needed $625, won $626 in the lottery only 24 hours after attending her first seminar. Larry Stone attracted so many new customers that he had to turn business away. Stephanie Coffin was thrilled to report that she completely overcame every symptom of MS (multiple sclerosis). Brooke Peterson went from feeling financially limited to earning over $300,000 in just six months (working only part time out of her home). There are many inspiring testimonials toward the end of this book (beginning on page 113) that

13

will offer you an enormous sense of hope and encouragement. Even if only *one* person has been successful at accomplishing a particular thing, **you can do it too.** If it has never been done before, then *you* can be the first!

4. ***How long does it take before I am likely to see positive results?***

You are likely to experience a positive effect *immediately*! You'll notice how good you feel right away, which encourages you to consistently claim 15 minutes a day to actually *do* this process. Doing it *daily* seems to produce the best results! It's usually only a short time before an abundance of "incredible coincidences" magically begin to show up in your life on a regular and predictable basis.

5. ***What does The 15-Minute Miracle primarily teach?***

It teaches us how to easily connect with that intuitive aspect of ourselves that knows only **answers and solutions**. It playfully invites us to discover our *highest thought* (**joy**), our *clearest word* (**Truth**) and our *grandest feeling* (**l♥ve**). Since Life communicates with us through our thoughts and feelings, we can learn to interpret them in a way that serves to keep us on a smooth and steady course. Although this process is quite compatible with most common belief systems, I suggest that you think of it as a giant smorgasbord of creative ideas—just fill your plate with whatever seems delicious to you!

6. ***What makes it different from other self-help programs?***

The biggest difference is the **simplicity and ease** with which a person can apply it and *benefit* from it. Because this process is *solution* oriented, it is presented from a purely positive perspective. It naturally inspires a feeling of exhilaration, encouragement, and positive anticipation. The basic principles behind 𝕿𝖍𝖊 15-𝕸𝖎𝖓𝖚𝖙𝖊 𝕸𝖎𝖗𝖆𝖈𝖑𝖊 are certainly not new—only the ease with which we can rapidly integrate these ideas into our lives is unique.

7. ***Is it anything like meditation?***

Although it certainly renders the wonderful *benefits* of meditation, it requires less time, and it's much more playful. It's more like a pleasurable form of "contemplation." I was always eager to follow my bliss as Drs. Wayne Dyer and Deepak Chopra suggested. I longed to master the ancient art of meditation, but I had great difficulty in *quieting* my busy mind. Furthermore, I was totally unsuccessful at *focusing* upon my breathing and *thinking* of "nothing!"

The 15-Minute ✦Miracle was a perfect way for me to access and "follow my bliss," because it only took 15 minutes a day to achieve incredible joy and well-being. It worked remarkably well for me, because I was able to *consciously* engage in something that made me happy on *all* levels of consciousness.

8. ***Can I learn this technique by just reading this book, or must I attend one of the playshops?***

It has been my experience that most anyone can learn this solution-oriented technique very quickly by merely reading this book and applying the simple principles. If, however, you wish to *accelerate* the rate at which you experience the kind of results that dreams are made of, you would greatly benefit from attending one of the weekend playshops. It's fun to walk through each concept just one step at a time until you thoroughly understand the entire process. These gatherings empower you with the kind of self-awareness that allows you to deliberately *manifest* things into your life with incredible ease. Even more than that, they make it easy for you to become fully connected (and *stay* connected) to a glorious state of mind that tends to take you beyond where you have ever been before. Attending a playshop is like taking a *shortcut* to *deliberately* creating your very own marvels, ✦Miracles, and incredible coincidences! It is our personal goal to consistently exceed your wildest expectations.

9. ***What exactly are you supposed to do for 15 minutes a day?***

The 15-Minute ✦Miracle consists of only *four* basic steps. You simply write down your answers to the four easy questions on page 21. It's best to write the very *first* thoughts that come into your mind, because they are accurate reflections of your truest feelings and deepest desires. You'll be quite amazed to see how fast your life takes a positive *shift.* As I always say…

"✦**Positive Shift Happens**"—and it can happen to you!

10. ***What is the best time of day to do this process?***

Some people find that doing it the very first thing in the morning works best for them, because it paves the way for them to enjoy their day in a more powerful and positive way. I, personally, prefer to do it just before I retire for the evening—that way, the positive possibilities that I am pondering have all night to gently settle into my subconscious. You can really do it at *any* time of day, but it's best to pick a time when you can set aside 15 minutes *for* yourself and *by* yourself! It's also a good idea to turn off the ringer on your phone, so you can enjoy your privacy even more. You can do The 15-Minute Miracle in the morning, the evening, or anytime in between. The most important thing is that you **just do it**! The sooner you begin, the sooner you'll see positive results!

11. ***What are the four simple steps?***

You can very easily learn all four steps by just reading this book and/or attending one of the empowering 15-Minute Miracle Playshops™ (you may call 1-888-468-4335 for the current schedules). You are in for a big treat when you begin to experiment with this playful and powerful process. Just wait until you see the miraculous events that *magically* begin to show up in your life!

*Though today is the **first** day of the rest of my life,*
*I choose to live it as though it were my **last**!*

Jacquelyn Aldana ✟ S.o.L.

Are you

Singing the **Song**

you came to **Sing**?

Joe and Judy Sabah

One of ✳ God's greatest ✳ Miracles is

to enable ✳ **Ordinary** people to

do ✳ **Extraordinary** things.

H. Jackson Brown, Jr.

Part 2

- The 15-Minute ✳ Miracle Formula

- ✳ Benefits of The 15-Minute ✳ Miracle

- Let's Tune in to ✳ Wiii FM (What is in it For Me?)

- ✳ IT Is Your Best Friend!

- What Do You Really Need to Be ✳ Happy?

- Valuable Coupon, ✳ Permission Slip, and ✳ A Round Tuit

✴ Formula

...an exact method, recipe,
or prescription intended to
express a fundamental
truth or principle.

The 15-Minute ✳ Miracle Formula

What do I ✳ **Appreciate**?

How do I desire to ✳ **Feel**?

What do I ✳ **Choose** *to do?*

What shall I **Ask** ✳ **Life to Provide**
for me today?

If you can just answer these four simple questions,

you can quickly attract and create many marvels,

✳ Miracles, and extraordinary coincidences

into your life with incredible ease.

✴ Benefits

… advantages that offer
us a sense of well-being. ✴ Life
continually offers us a multitude
of benefits, but it is up to us to become
aware of them, so we can *accept*
them into our lives.

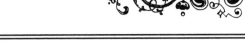

Benefits of
The 15-Minute ✳ Miracle

...as expressed by enthusiastic readers

Makes me ✳ happy!

Improves my ✳ health!

Increases my ✳ self-worth!

Makes me feel closer to ✳ God!

Empowers me with ✳ confidence!

Allows me to feel in ✳ control of my life!

Lets me ✳ appreciate myself unconditionally!

✳ Eliminates the need to worry about anything!

Allows me to greatly **increase** *my ✳ income at will!*

Gently guides me toward my highest and best ✳ good!

Provides abundant ✳ energy for me to do whatever I desire!

Gives me ✳ permission to focus upon things that make me happy!

Inspires me to do even ✳ greater things than I ever dreamed possible!

Greatly improves ✳ relationships with my mate, co-workers, and friends!

Offers a foolproof formula for turning not-so-good days into ✳ great days!

If you ✴ **Know**

what you ✴ **Want**

you can ✴ **Have** it!

R.H.J., author of *It Works*

Let's Tune in to ✴**Wiii FM**
(**W**hat **i**s **i**n **i**t **F**or **M**e?)

*Mentally check off the adjectives that best describe how **you** like to feel.*

_ Optimistic	_ Empowered	_ Prosperous	_ Self-confident
_ Blissful	_ Affluent	_ Lighthearted	_ Accomplished
_ Unlimited	_ Energetic	_ Positive	_ Exhilarated
_ Powerful	_ Dynamic	_ Delighted	_ Appreciated
_ Enthusiastic	_ Fulfilled	_ Elated	_ Ecstatic
_ Worthy	_ Invigorated	_ Focused	_ Beautiful
_ Content	_ Mentally Sharp	_ Strong	_ Spirited
_ Physically Fit	_ Passionate	_ Creative	_ Awesome
_ Attractive	_ Inspired	_ Desirable	_ Exceptional
_ Intuitive	_ Happy	_ Peaceful	_ Steady
_ Motivated	_ Exuberant	_ Aware	_ Playful
_ Balanced	_ Harmonious	_ Extraordinary	_ Romantic
_ Productive	_ Youthful	_ Articulate	_ Adventurous
_ Self-assured	_ Generous	_ L♥ving	_ Serene
_ Courageous	_ Flexible	_ Healthy	_ Joyful
_ Talented	_ Humorous	_ Comfortable	_ Lucky
_ Vivacious	_ Wholesome	_ Spontaneous	_ Versatile
_ Capable	_ Complete	_ Proficient	_ Calm
_ Independent	_ Free	_ Thrilled	_ Spiritual
_ Clear	_ Inventive	_ Progressive	_ Vital
_ Receptive	_ Jovial	_ Clever	_ Carefree
_ Secure	_ Special	_ Responsive	_ Wise

*The more items you are drawn to, the more potential
you have to benefit from 𝕿𝖍𝖊 15-Minute ✴Miracle process!*

IT

is your

Invisible **T**eacher.

Jacquelyn Aldana ✳ S.o.L.

✳ **IT** Is Your **Best Friend!**

𝕿𝖍𝖊 15-𝕸𝖎𝖓𝖚𝖙𝖊 ✳𝕸𝖎𝖗𝖆𝖈𝖑𝖊 teaches us how to effectively communicate with our ✳Invisible Teacher (affectionately known as ✳IT). ✳IT is that "inner voice" that speaks to us to offer guidance from time to time. It's easy to recognize this voice, because ✳IT always encourages us to move forward (*toward* our highest and best good). ✳IT is essentially the same as our ✳InTuition. Someone once told me that intuition is really ✳**God speaking to us between our thoughts**. If this is true, perhaps I'll *talk* a little less and *listen* a lot more!

✳Life cleverly communicates with us through our thoughts, feelings, and emotions. Sometimes we get messages in the form of pictures or images in our minds, while at other times we experience a strong *feeling* or a *hunch* about something. If you want to skillfully interact with your divine nature, it is in your best interest to pay very close attention to the way you *feel* about things. The more you consciously notice what you are feeling and experiencing, the easier it will be for you to access desired answers and solutions whenever you choose.

You'll be glad to know that every situation offers a benefit of some kind. It is actually a blessing when you experience that twinge of negative emotion from time to time. It's only ✳Life letting you know that you are *temporarily* out of harmony with your desires. That's your cue to *immediately* turn all of your attention to something you *appreciate*. A simple sense of gratitude inspires you to feel optimistic right away! When you realize that your ✳Invisible Teacher is merely prompting you to focus upon things that make you happy, you will be able to more easily accept whatever ✳Life offers you (*regardless* of conditions). When you discover how to effectively communicate with ✳IT,

> *you'll be able to* **be, do,** *or* **have** *whatever you are*
> *willing to focus your attention upon* **easily and effortlessly.**

Once we discover how we *unknowingly* attract undesirable circumstances into our lives, we can then *deliberately* call forth the conditions we *prefer* to experience instead!

27

It's as easy as going shopping! You just make a list of what you *want* to buy, then you go to the store and *find* the items you *intend* to purchase. Notice that you don't make a list of everything you *don't* want—you only focus upon what you *do* want when you go shopping.

At first, you may be somewhat skeptical of this "sounds-too-good-to-be-true" process. I don't blame you! Because it's so easy, it is hard to imagine how it can actually work so quickly (and with so little effort). I don't expect you to truly comprehend the power of *The 15-Minute ✳Miracle* until you actually do it and experience it for yourself. Once you see what happens, you'll better understand why so many people have become so fascinated with it. Many who have already experienced the magic of this irresistible process enthusiastically exclaim …

"✳IT works! ✳IT really works!"

That's why I have every reason to believe that ✳IT will work for you as well. As you read this book, you will see the word ✳IT many times. Every time you see or hear this word, please remember what ✳IT really is. ✳IT is the *Divine Presence* within us that creates the conscious awareness of the many possibilities that are available to us—✳IT is our ✳Invisible Teacher who absolutely adores us. It's especially comforting to know that …

✳IT is always with us.

There is only one time when ✳IT *appears* to be absent. When we are negatively focused upon problems or self-pity, ✳IT *seems* to be nowhere around. When, however, we decide to take responsibility for our lives and begin to look for solutions, we can't get rid of ✳IT! The funny thing is…the more we freely enjoy ✳IT and have fun with ✳IT, the better ✳IT works!

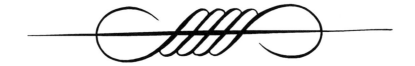

What Do **You** Really **Need** to Be **Happy**?

To keep this process light and uplifting, Ron suggested I provide you with the tools that will make getting started extremely easy. The majority of people we surveyed wanted very much to find a way to enjoy life more; however, they consistently told us that they were waiting to obtain *three* things. They typically said,

"When I get enough **time***,*
when I get **permission***,*
and when I get **around to it***,*

…then I will be able to be happy!" Often we limit ourselves, because we *believe* we require these three things before we *deserve* to experience a sense of well-being! A shortcut to realizing your dreams and desires is to **give yourself permission** to do the things you l♥ve most—things that generate life-force energy, boost your immune system, and cause you to leap out of bed in the morning with unstoppable enthusiasm! When you do what you truly *enjoy* doing, then l♥ve, prosperity, and ☀Miracles have no choice but to follow you everywhere! This is definitely one of ☀Life's best kept secrets!

If you relate to any of the above "reasons why I can't enjoy life now," you have come to the right place. Included in this book (at no extra charge) are all three things you need in order to take quantum leaps into a happier, more fulfilling life. Feel free to use these tools as often as you like. They are good for an entire lifetime, so you can take advantage of them whenever you like. Go ahead…

Allow yourself to **be playful** *and* **have fun** *with this!*

✳ Valuable Coupon

This coupon entitles the bearer to ✳ 15 Minutes per day
for the purpose of attracting ✳ Miracles!

This time is reserved exclusively for you, and **only you!**
It's guaranteed ☺**Guilt-Free,** ☺**Fat-Free,** and ☺**Totally Legal!**

✳ Permission Slip

Unconditional **permission is now granted,** hereby enabling you to **feel free to**…
(Please check off that which applies to you, and use the blank lines to write in additional requests.)

__ Goof off	__ Take a day off	__ Spend money on yourself
__ Take a nap	__ Listen to music	__ Eat whenever you want to
__ Laugh a lot	__ Take a vacation	__ Take time out just for you
__ Fall in l♥ve	__ Go to bed early	__ Honestly say what you feel
__ Take a walk	__ Appreciate yourself	__ Treat yourself to a massage
__ Take a break	__ Have fun and be happy	__ Sleep in until you feel rested
__ Read a book	__ Spend quiet time alone	__ Take time to do nothing at all
__ Watch a movie	__ Lighten up and enjoy life	__ Meditate and think of nothing
__ Breathe deeply	__ Release, let go, and relax	__ Do your 15-Minute ✳ Miracle
_____	_____	_____

Note: You are **entitled** to only as much permission as you are **willing** to accept!

Void if accompanied by Guilt, Fear, or Anxiety!   ♥   Permission Slip expires when you do!

Now you can **Do It!**

Part 3

- What We ✴ Think About is What We ✴ Bring About

- The Law of ✴ Magnetic Attraction

- Why the ✴ Rich Get ✴ Richer and the Poor Get Poorer

- Why The 15-Minute ✴ Miracle Works

- ✴ Free Will = ✴ Freedom

 **Thought**

…an idea, concept, intention, or
belief. Thoughts are definitely *things!*
We *become* what we think about through The
Law of Magnetic Attraction. We *invite* each and
every circumstance we encounter through
the thoughts we *choose* to think.

What We ✦ Think About
Is What We ✦ Bring About

We automatically invite every single experience we have through the focus of our attention. This is a rule to which there are no exceptions. If we *choose* to focus upon a **problem**, our invitation might read:

Attention All Problems and Negative Influences:

The Honor of Your Presence is Requested in the Life of

_____

Please come immediately, and bring along all of your close relatives, namely...

Pain

Fear

Guilt

Anger

Stress

Illness

Anxiety

Resentment

Lack and Limitation

...And the Rest of the Gang.

This could very well be the biggest **Pity Party** *you've attended all year!*

Conversely, when we choose to focus upon **solutions**, our invitation might resemble this:

Attention All ✦ Solutions and ✦ Positive Aspects!

The Honor of Your Presence is Requested in the Life of

_____

I dearly l♥ve, admire, and appreciate each one of you. You are encouraged to bring along all of your close friends, relatives, and associates, namely…

Joy

L♥ve

Light

Peace

Beauty

Wisdom

Courage

Harmony

Happiness

Well-Being

Confidence

Prosperity

Abundance

Motivation

Inspiration

Perfect Health

Please plan to **Stay Forever**, as there is only ✦ **Unconditional L♥ve** here for you.

The Law of  Magnetic Attraction

Life's Most Powerful Universal Law!

Thoughts are magnetic and *attract*
whatever you *choose* to focus your attention upon.

You will **Never, Never** attract the ☺**Solution**
while you are focused upon the ☹**Problem**!

You will never attract...	While you are focused upon...
✦ L♥VE	...FEAR
✦ HAPPINESS	...SORROW
✦ FREEDOM	...LIMITATION
✦ ABUNDANCE	...SCARCITY
✦ ENERGY	...LETHARGY
✦ PEACE OF MIND	...ANXIETY
✦ SUCCESS	...FAILURE
✦ CONFIDENCE	...UNWORTHINESS
✦ WELL-BEING	...WORRY
✦ SECURITY	...VULNERABILITY
✦ HARMONY	...RESISTANCE
✦ WELLNESS	...ILLNESS
✦ COMPANIONSHIP	...LONELINESS
✦ PROSPERITY	...POVERTY
✦ FORGIVENESS	...RESENTMENT

I've been ✦Rich,

and I've been **Poor**—

✦**Rich is Better**!

Mae West

Why the ✴ Rich Get ✴ Richer and the Poor Get Poorer

Have you ever wondered why some people seem to be very successful in life in terms of l♥ving relationships, good health, and prosperity, while others seem to have nothing but problems in one or more of these areas? Coming just a little closer to home…have you ever wondered why *you* sometimes get what you really want in life, and at other times you feel as though you are…

a **victim** *of circumstance?*

To successfully draw positive results into our lives *on purpose,* we must first understand how we *unknowingly* attract what we *don't* want, to better understand how we can *deliberately* call forth what we *do* want! This single awareness provides us with a valuable gift more precious than all the gold in Fort Knox.

When I first became aware of how I received my so-called "lot in life," I experienced a rather rude awakening that left me feeling quite uncomfortable. As you read the next paragraph, please know that it is natural to feel somewhat taken aback at first; however, when you read further, you will discover why this revelation is such a valuable insight.

The shocking news is…we actually attract what we *don't* want, as well as what we *do* want, simply by the way we choose to think and feel about things. Anything we say **"Yes"** to, we naturally *invite* into our life experience. Likewise, whatever we say **"No"** to, we *also* invite into our life experience! In other words, whatever we choose to focus our attention upon (whether it's something we *want* or something we want to get *rid* of), we automatically and *unavoidably* summon it into our physical reality. In other words, **we are the cause of our own experiences**—both positive *and* negative! I'm certainly not implying we *intentionally* attract undesirable experiences; however, we absolutely *do* attract them! For that matter, we seldom *deliberately* call forth our positive experiences either. If we neglect to deliberately *choose* what we prefer in life, we are unable to purposely *attract* that which we desire. Whatever we fix our attention upon is the very thing we can expect to bring into being. Therefore, it is in our best interest to consistently *visualize* that which offers us a sense of upliftment (instead of dwelling on things that worry us). If "what is" does not please you very much, then consciously *shift* your attention, and deliberately *focus* upon "how you would *prefer* things to be."

The good news is…since we are responsible for attracting our own life experiences (both good *and* bad), we can actually summon whatever we truly desire in life *on purpose;* that is, if we are willing to focus our attention (and intention) upon it long enough! The ability to *deliberately* attract circumstances and conditions to ourselves has wonderful benefits—it means we can use our thoughts to *intentionally* improve the quality of our lives. It means we are not victims and that nothing can really hold power over us without our consent! It is so exciting to realize that all conditions in our lives are nothing more than expressions of our thoughts and feelings. What we think about really *is* what we bring about!

"The rich get richer" because they have a tendency to focus upon prosperity and solutions…and in doing so, they get more of these things. "The poor get poorer" because they are inclined (due to their fear of scarcity) to focus primarily upon poverty and problems. The bad news is that they can only attract the very things they fear most. The good news is that **FEAR** (according to the delightful singer, David Roth) is really just an acronym for "**F**orgetting **E**verything's **A**ll **R**ight." The bottom line is this: when we are negatively focused, we can only continue to see more evidence of lack and limitation. Both scenarios are perfect examples of The Law of Magnetic Attraction in action! Remember…this immutable universal law is always working either *for* us or *against* us—how it works is all based upon how we simply *choose* to focus our attention! Think and focus only upon *abundance* and *prosperity* today, and just…

notice *what you* **attract** *and* **create**!

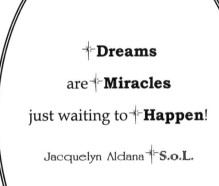

⁺Dreams

are ⁺**Miracles**

just waiting to ⁺**Happen**!

Jacquelyn Aldana ⁺**S.o.L.**

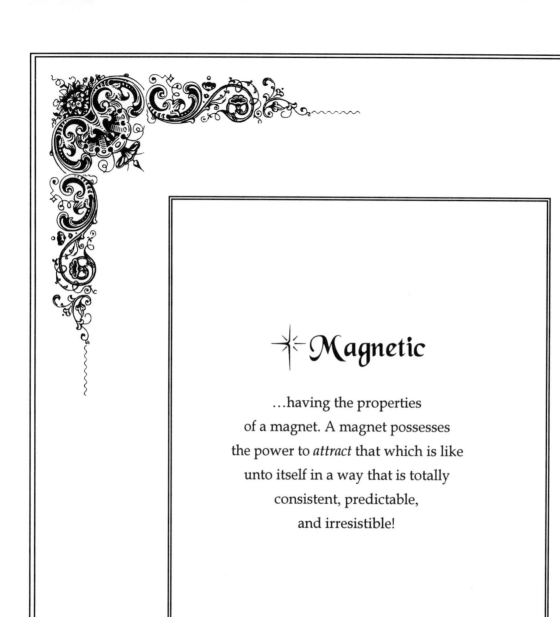

✳ Magnetic

…having the properties
of a magnet. A magnet possesses
the power to *attract* that which is like
unto itself in a way that is totally
consistent, predictable,
and irresistible!

Why
The 15-Minute ✦ Miracle
Works

By simply understanding The Law of Magnetic Attraction and how to *allow* it to work in our favor, we can *deliberately* attract whatever life experiences we *choose*. Like any universal law, it is totally impersonal and operates every minute of every day. **There are no exceptions**! When it comes to consciously *choosing* what happens to us in life, it truly *is* the most powerful law in the entire ✦ Universe!

The creation of all things begins with a thought—nothing more than just a manifestation of your imagination. Every thought is a powerful form of energy with its own unique vibrational frequency. Think of yourself as a transmitter and ✦ Life as a receiver. As you *think, speak,* and *feel* you silently project a radio-like signal, which ✦ Life then interprets as a request for physical manifestation. It has no choice but to deliver circumstances that match the frequency of your *thoughts, words,* and *feelings*. You have the power to determine what your life experiences will be in the future based upon what you have *chosen* think about now. Although thoughts begin as invisible, non-physical things, they ultimately become tangible, physical realities.

Our **thoughts** *are incredibly* **powerful magnets**!

A thought irresistibly attracts all other thoughts and conditions that are in harmony with itself, just like a piece of magnetite (magnetic iron ore) naturally attracts iron. This is why our thoughts can make such a *tremendous* difference in how our lives turn out. Where we are now is a result of what we have thought about in the past! To quote Ralph Waldo Emerson…"The ancestor of every action is a thought."

It's exciting to realize that we can enhance our lives by simply enhancing the way we think! As we merely think or speak a particular thought, it actually becomes

BIGGER! This is comparable to the phenomenon that takes place when we position a magnifying glass so the light from the sun is steadfastly focused upon a sheet of paper. The sun generates so much energy (in the form of heat) that it can't help but result in **spontaneous combustion**—so it is with our thoughts and feelings. The more we *focus* upon a particular condition, the more energy we attract to it. It becomes so **amplified** and **e x p a n d e d** that it finally *ignites* into a physical reality!

Since what we think about actually enlarges each time we contemplate it, we greatly benefit by *focusing* our thoughts only upon those things that we truly *want* to experience in our lives. Concentrating upon things we wish to avoid is like deciding to go shopping and making a list of everything we don't want! That is a sure way to accumulate an enormous amount of unwanted garbage in our lives. Every time you choose to worry about something, you are automatically *asking* for it to become an active part of your experience. Is this what you really want?

Thoughts have a tremendous amount of very real *power* to draw our life experiences to us in the form of physical realities. Fortunately, we have *control* over what we think—we can consciously *choose* that which we ponder in our minds. Mere thoughts can allow us to become *well* or cause us to become *ill*. We can summon *prosperity* into our lives just as quickly as we can attract *poverty*. What we experience depends upon how we *choose* to focus our attention. Since we are able to *choose* our thoughts, we can also *influence* our circumstances. Now that you realize this, just think of all that you can do!

When you experience a positive thought, your body absolutely *thrives*. Your magnificent internal pharmacy magically produces a multitude of wonderful immune-boosting chemicals and hormones such as interferon, interleukins, and endorphins. These substances are natural drugs produced by your own body. They are endowed with powerful, health-enhancing properties that automatically *supercharge* your immune system. In fact, endorphins are one of nature's analgesics. They relieve physical pain, because (according to scientific studies) they are actually **four times more potent than morphine**. I suggest you read *Anatomy of an Illness* by Norman Cousins to better understand the amazing healing power of laughter (he literally laughed himself well)!

When you think negative thoughts (thoughts of resistance related to fear, anger, or resentment), your body can only produce toxic chemicals that greatly *suppress* your immune system. Dr. Deepak Chopra, a well-known author and endocrinologist, claims that our blood can actually become *lethal* when we experience strong negative emotions. It has been scientifically proven that just a couple of drops of this toxic blood injected into a healthy hamster can kill it *immediately!* In fact, a mother experiencing extreme negative emotions (fear, anger, or rage) unavoidably passes deadly chemicals into her breast milk, which can seriously jeopardize the health of her nursing baby. Just imagine how we are poisoning our bodies with our prolonged *toxic thinking*. This explains why we usually get sick when we are least happy about life. Have you noticed how tired and lethargic you become when things aren't going your way?

When you're out of **harmony**, *you're out of* **energy**!

The universal Law of Magnetic Attraction is operating at all times. Even as we contemplate this idea, this omnipresent force is either working *for* us or *against* us. It works incessantly. Which way it affects our lives, however, is entirely up to *us*. It matters not that we understand it or even believe in it—it works *regardless* of all that. The trick is to find out how to allow it to work in *harmony* with us! When you take the time to understand the basic principles behind The Law of Magnetic Attraction, you can easily **take charge of your life** in a way that will generate a tremendous sense of confidence and well-being within you.

When you are confident and happy, you are able to see the positive aspects of life much more easily. As you focus upon *these* things, they become your *new* points of attraction. Whatever you allow to dominate your attention is what you can expect to attract and experience. In other words, you have a great deal of influence with regard to your personal destiny! You are much more powerful that you probably realize.

✴ Free Will

…the divine freedom to
consciously *choose* what we
truly desire to be, do,
have, or believe.

✴ Free Will = ✴ **Freedom**

We are so fortunate to be alive at this particular time to enjoy the pure and wonderful quality of life called *freedom*—total freedom to think, feel, and experience whatever our hearts desire. It is believed to be a *divine gift* from ✴God and is most commonly referred to as "**free will.**" This splendid attribute enables us to make our *own* choices—in fact, creative expression is highly encouraged. Free will is so pristine that we have even been given the choice to appreciate (or not appreciate) the generous *Source* of this l♥ving gift. This is an example of unconditional l♥ve at its best!

It's truly ✴Life's pleasure to provide each one of us with all the tools we need to achieve our goals. It is up to us, however, to *discover* the tools and figure out how to use them. If we can clearly *identify* that which delights us, ✴Life will gladly provide it. When we merely ponder thoughts of appreciation, we *automatically* invite desirable results into our lives. Sincere **appreciation** is a cordial **invitation** to deliberate **creation**. When we remember that we are divine extensions of ✴The L♥ving Power that Created All That Is, we naturally enjoy a sense of worthiness and begin to look forward to good things to come. We only need to keep our hearts and arms wide open to *accept* that which we desire!

When we ask for things to come to us in just the perfect time and in ways that benefit everyone concerned, it is easier for us to release our attachment to the outcome and trust that ✴Life will support us. We are able to enjoy a sense of abundance when we believe (beyond a shadow of a doubt) that there is a plenitude of all things in the ✴Universe and that our needs are always met. Our only work is to *decide* what we want, and ✴Life will be eager to provide it. In other words, our job is to figure out what makes our heart sing—✴Life's job is to *orchestrate* the details and *deliver* the object of our desires. Ah-h-h-h! What a magnificent system!

In order to help us make decisions, ✴Life provided us with another valuable gift known as "contrast." Contrast is absolutely *essential* to our lives, as it provides a frame of reference that enables us to make conscious *choices*. Typically, we develop definite *preferences* for things as we experience various aspects of life. We quickly find out that we prefer to be *warm* when we are cold, *well* when we are ill, and *happy* when we are sad. When we stand next to a small child, we become aware that we are quite *large* by comparison. In the presence of an elephant, however, we realize just how *small* we really are. As we experience life and make comparisons, we begin to understand that we live in a ✳Universe where everything is actually just *relative* to everything else. In other words, there is **no need to judge anything**, as nothing is necessarily good or bad, more or less, better or worse, etc. (except through our own *perception* of it).

What do we mean by "perception?" Perception is merely our mental grasp of an idea gained through our various senses. Our individual view points are based upon our personal life experiences…and since our experiences vary a great deal, so do our perceptions. For example, it's interesting to note how various people perceive death. To a doctor, death may be equivalent to *failure,* while death to the soul may be an enormous *relief.* To the l♥ved ones left behind, death can be *devastating,* yet the mortician views death as an *opportunity* to procure another customer! The person who dies very likely experiences a welcomed sense of *peace* and *relief* as he (she) finally releases all resistance to the conditions of life! As Albert Einstein once said, "Either *nothing* is a ✳Miracle, or *everything* is a ✳Miracle!" It all depends upon how we *perceive* that which we experience and what we *believe* to be true. A belief, by the way, is nothing more than a thought that we keep on thinking. Since your beliefs influence your life experiences, it's wise to selectively *choose* to maintain the ones that elevate your sense of well-being.

When our world is in perfect balance and harmony, things seem very, very good. Our lives are fun, easy, and remarkable in every way—we naturally feel free and happy. When, however, we begin to focus upon what we *don't want,* what we want to *get rid of,* and what is *wrong* with the world, our lives can feel pretty overwhelming at times. If our focus is upon fear and negativity, ✳Life has no choice but to deliver the very things we are afraid of and the things we don't want! Have you ever noticed that the person who consistently talks about how terrible life is, is the same person

who continues to see even *more* evidence of disharmony day after day? Remember…
what we choose to think about is what we *automatically* and *unavoidably* bring about!

Fortunately, we have the power to deliberately connect with a sense of well-being whenever we wish to. Since we are naturally creative beings, we have the innate resources to create whatever qualities we *choose* to invite into our lives. Have you ever heard the expression, "All men (people) were created equal?" I never really understood what this meant until I realized that we *all* have the same power to choose our thoughts, *regardless* of prevailing conditions! The one freedom that we *all* have is the freedom to *choose* what we think about! Regardless of circumstances, we are still the masters of our thoughts. Since what we think about influences what we experience, we can therefore enjoy a degree of predictability with regard to what happens to us in life! When we intentionally *choose* our thoughts, we deliberately *choose* our destiny. From this standpoint, we were *all* born free! **All you have to do is exercise your freedom of choice**—simply think about whatever you desire to attract and experience!

"That's much easier *said* than done!" you may be thinking to yourself. Before The 15-Minute ✝Miracle became a way of life for me, I would have probably said the very same thing. At this time, however, I want to assure you that regaining your balance and finding joy in life is "just as easily *done* as said." The only prerequisite to your success is to have a sincere *desire* to feel good—the desire to remember who you really are (the "✝Magnificent Creation" in whom your ✝L♥ving Creator is well pleased)! One of the quickest and most enjoyable ways to accomplish this is to give yourself permission to take **just 15 minutes a day** to playfully experiment with the magical little process called The 15-Minute ✝Miracle. It quickly enables you to reconnect to the *peace* of mind and the *passion* for life that inspires your reason for being! It reminds you that we are *all* creative and gifted in some way (and you are no exception).

When you consciously decide to experience life from a joyous and positive perspective, you are able to enjoy that inexplicable feeling of "coming home." This is the best way I know to describe what it feels like to be fully "connected" to ✝Life. To truly *live,* you must consciously *choose* to live! You must have a definite *desire* to be joyful and look forward to the infinite possibilities that ✝Life has to offer. If you want to be *happy,* you have to *choose* to be happy! This is the first step toward realizing your fondest dreams and desires—the rest of the process is even easier!

At this point, I suggest that you **get ready to fall in l♥ve** with all of the positive possibilities that are available to you just for the asking! As Plato said, "There is a place that *you* are to fill that no one else can fill—something *you* are to do that no one else can do." It took several life challenges and over half a century for me to recognize *my* unique talent. I instantly recognized it when I discovered The 15-Minute ☀ Miracle a few years ago. I found it was very easy for me to gather infinite amounts of eternal knowledge and distill it into something very *convenient* and *easy* to use. It was like rounding up the wisdom of the ages and placing it in a funnel the size of the ☀ Universe. What magically flowed through the small opening of this funnel was an amazing vortex of understanding —a crystal-clear awareness of the universal laws that enable *all* of us to deliberately attract and create our own life experiences. This illuminating perception is like having a sparkling jewel that is small enough to hold in your hand, put in your pocket, and take with you everywhere!

I now invite you to join me on a delightful adventure that offers a *shortcut* to discover *your* divine gift more easily. The 15-Minute ☀ Miracle offers you the perfect **ROAD MAP** (**R**eally **O**utstanding **A**nd **D**elightful ☀ **M**iracle **A**ttraction **P**rocess). By just engaging in this creative process for only 15 minutes a day, you can attract a wonderful awareness of whatever you want to know, feel, be, do, or have! It's a convenient *vehicle* that has the potential to take you from where you are right now, to places *beyond* where you have ever been before. By the way…if for any reason you wish to take *more* than 15 minutes a day to harness the magic of synchronicity, please feel perfectly free to do so. We promise that no one will summon the "☀ Miracle Police!"

You have now reached the part of the book that has the potential to greatly enhance the rest of your life in a way that will amaze and delight you. If you want to learn how to attract more joy, well-being, and abundance into your life, we invite you to embark upon an intriguing journey filled with infinite possibilities. Just know that ☀ Miracles are truly yours for the asking—but first you must ask!

Toward the end of this book (starting on page 113) there are several heart-warming stories that you may relate to in a personal way. I encourage you to read the "**Amazing✢Miracles that Touch the ♥Heart and Tickle the Soul**." These true-life testimonials are from everyday people (like you and me) who are simply playing with 𝕿𝖍𝖊 15-𝔐inute✢𝔐iracle and discovering how absolutely *magical* life can be day after day. These individuals thoughtfully shared their enriching stories to inspire and uplift *you*. As you experience encouraging results, please remember that *your* personal examples could offer tremendous upliftment and inspiration to *others*. That is why we invite you to become a valuable contributor and take just 15 minutes to write or call us **TOLL FREE** at *1-(888) In The Flow* (1-888-468-4335) to tell us about your ✢Miracles.

You *could make a*
Big Difference
in someone else's life!

If you want to ✦**Real-ize** it,

just simply ✦**Miracle-ize** it!

Heathcliff Aldana ✦**S.o.L.**

Part 4

- Step #1—Discover the Awesome Power of ☀ Appreciation

- Step #2—Decide Exactly How You Would L♥ve to ☀ Feel Today

- Step #3—Now ☀ Choose to Experience Whatever ☀ Delights You

- Step #4—Invite Assistance from ☀ The Creator of All That Is

- The Seven Secrets of Success

- My 15-Minute ☀ Miracle (Example)

- ☀ Positive Perceptions and ☀ Playful Possibilities

Appreciation

...grateful recognition,
evaluation of worth, and a warm
expression of admiration
and approval.

Discover the Awesome Power of ✳ Appreciation

The Attitude of Gratitude

The very first step in manifesting your own ✳ Miracles is to clearly understand the significant role that simple appreciation plays in your being able to deliberately attract desirable results. Did you know that it's virtually *impossible* to experience a negative emotion while you are appreciating anything or anyone? Notice how positive and uplifted you feel as you become aware of something to appreciate. Observe how your body relaxes and how you actually feel lighter. So many people tell us that they experience **an immediate sense of well-being** whenever they merely express their thankfulness. Have you ever noticed that when you offer your heartfelt appreciation to anyone, that you *automatically* experience a reciprocal flow of positive energy? In other words, you seem to receive the same wonderful sense of good will that you are offering to someone else!

It may really surprise you to discover that you can often favorably influence the behavior of *others* just through your appreciation of them. The results are positively magical! When you appreciate someone (even without them consciously knowing you are doing it), they are naturally inclined to respond to you in a much more positive manner. Once I listed all the *positive aspects* of a person with whom I had a major conflict. Within just half a day, he became one of my closest friends. Appreciation is far more powerful than most of us realize!

Have you ever noticed when someone sincerely appreciates you, that you just *instinctively* want to show much greater consideration for that person? This is commonly referred to as "**The Attitude of Gratitude.**" As we often say to acknowledge those whom we appreciate: "You're great and we're grateful!" If you want to feel good in a hurry, just find something (or someone) to appreciate.

What we appreciate quickly **e x p a n d s**. ✦Life humorously imitates my eager-to-please grandmother when she used to serve dinner. If I complimented her on a particular dish that she had l♥vingly prepared, she would *instantly* provide me with **second helpings!** ✦Life does exactly the same thing—it always makes sure that we get *more* of whatever we appreciate. The next time you want to deliberately summon something into your life, it may be fun to go ahead and offer sincere appreciation for it as you ponder the possibility of attracting it. The results are often quite amazing!

Let's start with **Step #1** of 𝕿𝖍𝖊 15-𝔐inute ✦𝔐iracle process. Take just a few minutes to write down everything you can think of that you **appreciate** at this time. Just let the ideas flow, and write down the very *first* impressions that come into your mind until your thoughts of gratitude are complete. If you want to **magnify** the positive effects, **e x p a n d** your statements of appreciation by describing how each thing for which you are thankful improves your sense of well-being (see the examples below).

Today, I really **Appreciate**…, because it enables and/or inspires me to…*(emphasize benefits)*

- *I really* **Appreciate** *my good health,* because it enables me to *feel vital and energetic.*

- *I really* **Appreciate** *my awareness of The 15-Minute Miracle,* because it inspires me to *deliberately choose my life experiences with confidence!*

- *I really* **Appreciate** *beautiful music,* because it inspires me to *relax and enjoy life.*

Pause for just a moment, and take a nice, deep, relaxing breath. Now close your eyes, and notice how your body feels. Perhaps you feel *happy, inspired,* and/or *encouraged.* Acknowledge how you feel in words that are meaningful to *you.* The benefit of paying attention to how you feel right now is that you can make the correlation between what you *think* and how you *feel* (turn on your **PA** system and **Pay Attention**). If you feel good when you express appreciation, you may want to do it more often!

Before we move on to the next step, I want to tell you an inspiring story of what an expression of appreciation did for Gemma Bauer. You see, Gemma had suffered excruciating pain for well over ten years due to chronic rheumatoid arthritis. She had literally tried just about every remedy, treatment, and technique known to man, with little or no success. Needless to say, she was more than just a *little* disappointed and discouraged. With tears of hopelessness in her eyes, she reported that she had attempted to faithfully practice The 15-Minute Miracle process the year prior to attending the playshop. She only did it for a few days, however, because she saw no significant results. Gemma had become so used to experiencing failure with such a wide variety of remedies, that she figured this was just one more thing that didn't work.

It wasn't until she attended the playshop that I became aware that, while Gemma *thought* she was doing The 15-Minute Miracle, she had completely neglected to do the first step—the appreciation step. Unfortunately, **this is equivalent to trying to walk through a wall, instead of using the door.** There is enormous value for us in *each* of the steps. The combination of *all* of these building blocks is what makes it so incredibly powerful. Without a strong *foundation* (appreciation), the other three steps have nothing substantial to stand upon! If you did nothing more than this one step, you would experience a major positive difference in your life. Appreciation and bliss are very closely related, so if you want to "follow your bliss," just find something to appreciate!

Attending an all-day playshop was not easy for Gemma. I could see that it was all she could do to actively participate. Distracted by her physical pain, she couldn't even remember very much about the day. In fact, when her mate asked her about what she had learned, all she could do was cry. Her story of what happened from this point on, however, is truly heartwarming. Please refer to page 117 of the chapter entitled **"Amazing Miracles that Touch the ♥Heart and Tickle the Soul,"** and read all about what happened to Gemma once she began to do The 15-Minute Miracle in its entirety.

Now let's see what
The 15-Minute Miracle *can do for you!*

✴𝔉eelings

…the language of the
soul—positive or negative
reactions that we have to conditions.
✴**IT** (our ✴Invisible Teacher) communicates
with us through our *feelings* to show
us where the focus of our
attention is at all times.

step #2

Decide Exactly How You Would L♥ve to ✴ Feel Today

Positive Feelings Attract Positive Results

Clearly focus *all* of your attention upon how you would really l♥ve to *feel*. As you probably know by now, The Law of Magnetic Attraction is at work every single moment. Whatever we consistently focus upon is what we can expect to experience. While ✴**positive thinking** is essential to attracting ✴Miracles, it's actually the power of ✴**positive feeling** that is responsible for successfully drawing ✴**positive experiences** into our lives.

Has anyone ever said something to you that you knew they honestly didn't mean? If so, I'm sure you recognize that it's not the words, but rather the *feeling* behind the words that contain the *power* to deliberately attract and create results. It's like someone casually saying, "Hi! You look nice today," as opposed to someone who approaches you with enormous enthusiasm and exclaims, "Wow! You look absolutely fabulous! I can hardly take my eyes off of you!" Can you *feel* the tremendous difference? Feelings evoke one of *two* basic emotions:

Positive emotion, *which* **feels good** *and offers us* **comfort**.

Negative emotion, *which* **feels bad** *and offers us* **discomfort!**"

When we experience *positive* emotion (which is based upon l♥ve), we are usually quite content. This, of course, causes us to attract experiences that offer us a sense of *comfort*. The moment we experience a *negative* emotion, however, we begin to create a momentum of attraction in the opposite direction. This is because we are coming from a place of fear, which offers us a strong sense of *discomfort*. Fear robs us of all positive possibilities and can only cause us to flee, fight, faint, or freeze (e-e-e-k). The longer we *focus* upon things we *fear,* the more we *attract* conditions that cause us to be *uncomfortable.* You'll be relieved to know that **FEAR** is merely "**F**orgetting **E**verything's **A**ll **R**ight." To quickly diffuse fear, simply focus upon what you would *prefer* to experience and find lots of things to appreciate. Now gently close your eyes as you contemplate the following question. Take a deep breath…exhale slowly…and ask yourself…

"How do I **feel** *as I just* **imagine** *that I have total freedom to* **be**, **do,** *or* **have** *absolutely anything I* **choose** *in life?"*

Now think of as many adjectives as you can
to describe how you truly *feel.* These may include:

_ Free	_ Unlimited	_ Ecstatic	_ Prosperous
_ Grateful	_ Carefree	_ Uplifted	_ Dynamic
_ Relieved	_ Optimistic	_ Energetic	_ Enthusiastic
_ Empowered	_ L♥ving	_ Generous	_ Ecstatic
_ Thrilled	_ Blissful	_ Fulfilled	_ Lighthearted
_ Delighted	_ Confident	_ Joyful	_ Spontaneous
_ Invigorated	_ Exhilarated	_ Excited	_ Comfortable

Do you notice how much lighter and freer you feel? Perhaps you feel more *relaxed, relieved,* and/or *exhilarated.* As mentioned earlier, as you contemplate pleasant thoughts, your entire body becomes flooded with immune-boosting chemicals that are equivalent to synthetic mood-elevating drugs. In fact, the moment you feel a sense of exhilaration and joy, natural opiates inside your body begin to connect with special receptors. This results in your becoming naturally "high!" Furthermore, **it's totally free and perfectly legal!** This is an outstanding example of what positive emotion feels like! Isn't it wonderful? If you'd like to find a way to capture this feeling and be able to call it forth at will, you are going to l♥ve what 𝕿𝖍𝖊 15-𝕸𝖎𝖓𝖚𝖙𝖊 ✝ 𝕸𝖎𝖗𝖆𝖈𝖑𝖊 will do for you.

I now invite you to practice **Step #2.** Simply write down how you would l♥ve to feel and why. After you make your Statement of Desire, then **paint a colorful word picture** that describes how wonderful it would be to actually experience it. Notice how very inspired and empowered you begin to feel. This technique of focusing upon benefits can really speed up your manifestation process! It's amazing how uplifted you begin to feel right away! Since the cells of your body constantly eavesdrop on everything you think, say, and feel, they anticipate your intention and immediately respond to accommodate your every belief. You are likely to experience this phenomenon when you merely *think* of sucking on a lemon—you may begin to salivate *involuntarily!* Here are a few examples of how you might like to phrase *your* Statements of Desire:

I love to **Feel**…When I…, then I…, which enables me to…*(emphasize benefits)*

- *I love to* **Feel** *full of abundant energy to do anything I choose easily and effortlessly. When I have surplus energy, then I feel assured that I can be, do, or have absolutely anything I desire, which enables me to move forward with enormous confidence!*

- *It's fun to* **Feel** *extremely self-confident and know that I can easily deal with any situation that comes along, regardless of circumstances. When I feel sure of myself, then I have the strength and inner knowing that all is really well, which enables me to believe that everything will work out in just the perfect time and in the highest and best good of all concerned.*

- *I* **Feel** *excited about new opportunities that I have yet to create. When I anticipate seeing the benefits that Life has to offer, then I am able to embrace everyone and everything with a sense of eagerness, which enables me to feel "high on life" in every moment!*

Excellent!
You only have **two more steps** *to go!*

59

 **Choose**

...to make a selection
using our divine gift of free
will. If we want to attract positive
results, we only need to make conscious
choices based upon our deliberate
and positive intentions.

Now ✳ **Choose** to Experience ✳ **Whatever** ✳ **Delights You**!

"If you know what you want, you can have it!"

R.H.J., anonymous author of *It Works!*

If someone were to ask you right this moment, "What do you really want out of life?" would you have a clear and detailed answer? Could you expound spontaneously for at least 15 minutes to describe what *truly* inspires your soul to do the dance of joy? If you are like most of us, you would probably scratch your head and say something like, "Uh-h-h, I don't know—I just want to be happy." Perhaps you would say, "It would be nice to have…

- *a new* **home**,
- *a new* **car**, *and*
- *enough* **time** *and* **money** *to travel.*"

This type of response is quite typical. Now compare this scenario to going to a restaurant where you have an *unlimited* selection of wonderful things from which to choose. Your waitress brings you a menu and thoughtfully asks, "What can I bring you today?" You reply, "I don't know. I'm hungry, and I just want some food." Well, you are more than mildly shocked and disappointed when she brings you **leftover** "cream-of-lampshade soup" with "chocolate covered ants" for dessert. It works *exactly* the same way in everyday life. If you say, "I'm alive, and I just want some life experiences," ✳Life will swiftly bring you whatever is **left over**, and it may not be exactly what pleases you! If you don't articulate your preferences, you are doomed to live life by default—that means you get what ✳Life dishes out at random!

Now for some encouraging news—when you clearly *specify* what you **prefer to be**, what you **like to do**, and what you l♥ve to have, your old friend (The Law of Magnetic Attraction), goes right to work to bring you whatever you have focused your attention upon. Your job is simply to *recognize* it and be ready to *accept* it. As incredible as this sounds, **it actually works**! In fact, it works just as consistently and predictably as The Law of Gravity. If you cannot easily figure out exactly what you want, simply write down something like…

I now **Choose** *to…*When I…, then I…, which enables me to…*(emphasize benefits)*

- *I now* **Choose** *to discover what really makes my heart sing.* When I *consciously know what I want,* then I *can bask in the unlimited possibilities that are available to me,* which enables me to *easily attract a multitude of blessings into my life.*

In a very short time, creative ideas will begin to magically flow into your awareness, and you will be on your way to manifesting things and situations that offer you a wonderful sense of *joy* and *exhilaration.*

You'll be glad to know that there's even a *positive* effect to experiencing a *negative* emotion. It's really nothing more than our trusty intuition (our ✶Invisible Teacher or sixth sense) attempting to communicate with us in a way that we can benefit. When we experience *negativity* from time to time, it's very comforting to know that it's merely our **magnificent innate guidance system** intending to be of service to us. ✶IT is our familiar inner voice telling us that we are a little off balance and in conflict with that which we *really* want in life.

By briefly identifying what we *don't* want, we can more easily *clarify* our desires. It's perfectly okay to acknowledge what you *don't* want for the purpose of clearly identifying that which you *do* want (but only for a very short time). It's important to remember that the powerful Law of Magnetic Attraction is totally *impersonal* and has no choice but to bring you whatever you focus your attention upon; therefore, it's a good idea to focus primarily upon that which *pleases* you. If you dwell upon anything of a negative nature for very long, The Law of Magnetic Attraction can only bring you the very thing you don't want! Once you understand this, you can successfully attract whatever you really want in life *on purpose!* Isn't that exciting?

Here's another pearl of wisdom worth remembering: ✝Life is *incapable* of hearing the word *don't* when followed by the word *want.* "I *don't want* bad news" is actually interpreted by ✝Life as "I *want* bad news!" As a result, we are really attracting the very thing we wish to avoid every time we say we **don't want** something! Everything we attempt to **push away**, want to **get rid of**, or **say "no" to**, we automatically and unavoidably *invite* into our lives!

By now, you may be wondering if you have to consciously monitor your every thought in order to attract desirable results (that would be a full-time job)! Fortunately, you need not concern yourself with whether you are having a positive thought or a negative thought. All you have to do is simply notice how you *feel* based upon the emotions you are experiencing. Remember…there are only *two* basic categories of emotions—*positive* (l♥ve) and *negative* (fear). If you have a feeling of lightness and comfort, just enjoy the moment and go with the "flow" of pure, positive energy. If, however, you begin to feel that "lump of dread" welling up in your stomach (as your body tenses up), you can be sure you are experiencing negative emotion.

At first, you may think this is a bad thing, but there is a quick and easy way to successfully deal with it. What to do? The solution is extremely simple and makes you feel better almost *immediately.* First think of something (anything) that you *appreciate,* then focus all of your attention upon what makes you happy when you merely *think* about it. Finally, zero in on precisely how you would prefer to *feel.* Now just watch the ✝Miracles begin to show up in your life! You may wonder how anything so *simple* could be so *powerful!* Just experiment with this magical process and see for yourself. The only thing you have to lose is your negative emotion! With everything you have read about and practiced so far, I am quite certain you will find it easy to do **Step #3** of 𝕿𝖍𝖊 15-𝕸inute ✝𝕸iracle.

Just close your eyes…
take a deep, relaxing breath…
and say to yourself either silently or out loud…

"Today, **I Can Be** *whatever* **I Desire,**

I Can Do *anything* **I Believe** *I can do, and*

I Can Have *as much prosperity as* **I Am Willing** *to accept."*

Below are a couple of examples of how you can use this step to attract and create results that please you. After you read them a couple of times, practice writing one in your own words.

I now **Choose** *to…* When I…, then I…, which enables me to…*(emphasize benefits)*

- *I now* **Choose** *to accomplish all that I set out to do.* When I *complete things on my agenda,* then I *feel totally inspired, positive, and empowered,* which enables me to *enjoy a strong sense of well-being.*

- *I now* **Choose** *to have a lot of fun and find many things to laugh about.* When I *have a good laugh,* then I *find it very easy to just be myself,* which enables me to *feel refreshed, relaxed, and uplifted!*

After you write down what you **choose** to do (attract, create, discover, invite, experience, etc.), take a moment to *consciously* observe how you *feel.* I am willing to bet that you feel much better than you did *before* you started. By now, you are probably getting a pretty good idea of how empowering this process really is. Keep up the good work! You have now successfully completed the third step of 𝕿𝖍𝖊 15-Minute ✝ Miracle. You're almost home.

…only **one more step** *to go!*

Always ✳ **Look**

where you are **Going**,

as you will always ✳ **Go**

where you are **Looking**!

Jacquelyn Aldana ✳ **S.o.L.**

✳ The Creator of All That Is

A name given to ✳The Creator of all things,
in all times, and in all places. Some of the names
that are used to describe ✳The Creator of All That Is are…

✳Christ

✳Holy Spirit

✳Great Spirit

✳The Almighty

✳Universal Mind

✳Divine Oneness

✳Heavenly Father

✳Innate Intelligence

✳Allah, ✳Jehovah, ✳Yahweh, and

✳God.

Please feel free to *choose*
whatever name is most compatible with
your personal belief system.

Invite Assistance from ✳ The Creator of All That Is

Let ✳ Life Handle the Details!

This is my very favorite step in 𝕿𝖍𝖊 15-𝕸𝖎𝖓𝖚𝖙𝖊 ✳ 𝕸𝖎𝖗𝖆𝖈𝖑𝖊 process. Some people associate it with "The Power of Prayer," while others think it has more to do with "The Power of Thought"—I'm inclined to think that both concepts are equally correct! Nothing could be easier or more appropriate than calling upon that Higher ✳ Power that we perceive to be greater than we are. This is most helpful when dealing with those things that appear to be out of our *own* realm of influence. Since ✳ 𝕿𝖍𝖊 𝕮𝖗𝖊𝖆𝖙𝖔𝖗 𝖔𝖋 𝕬𝖑𝖑 𝕿𝖍𝖆𝖙 𝕴𝖘 successfully sees to it that the earth remains spinning on its axis and keeps the sun, the moon, and the stars in the sky day after day, it would be safe to assume that this omnipotent ✳ Power is quite capable of orchestrating things of great magnitude. We call upon the very same energy that created worlds when we invite unconditional l♥ve and unlimited support from this ✳ Creative Life Force!

If you have played with steps one through three, you probably realize that you are developing an amazing skill to *deliberately* attract many wonderful things and experiences into your life. Well, you had better hang on to your enthusiasm when you apply this next step! It is absolutely incredible what will begin to happen when you decide to **ask ✳ Life for a helping hand**!

Ron and I experienced relatively simple demonstrations at first by requesting convenient parking spaces on a regular basis. One day, however, we had a full day's work to do in only four hours, and we heard on the radio that the entire metropolitan area was gridlocked due to accidents and construction work. It was even suggested that we stay home unless it was absolutely necessary to be on the roads. Well, I simply wrote down this request:

> *I now choose to* **Invite Assistance** *from* The Loving Power that Created All That Is. Thank you, ___God___, for always being here for me. I so appreciate when things come to me in just the perfect time and in ways that totally delight me. I love knowing that opportunities are limitless and that all is really well. **Thank you for your support in providing the following things that I perceive to be beyond my *own* ability to achieve:**
>
> - *Ron and I so appreciate your unconditional love and unlimited support. We have extensive distance to cover today, and we would like to easily complete all of our business in time to keep our afternoon appointment at 1:00. We look forward to a positive solution that is in the highest and best good of all concerned.*

The most amazing thing happened! When we approached the first traffic jam on the highway where they were doing construction work, we were waved into the far right lane—they opened it up just as we got there. We must have passed at least 3,000 cars that were just sitting there in the left lane (one is not likely to win a popularity contest under these circumstances)! Soon after that, we reached another impasse—this time, we were in the middle lane of traffic. It literally looked like "the parting of the Red Sea" as cars in front of us swiftly moved into either the right or the left lanes, allowing us to go through with incredible ease. When we came to the next standstill, *everyone* began moving forward—this whole experience was amazing! **We finished our work with time to spare!** This is a wonderful demonstration of what happens when you summon Divine Assistance. This final step is definitely one of the most awe-inspiring steps in The 15-Minute Miracle process.

I often use this step to request things of enormous magnitude, such as peace and harmony among all people. I primarily use it, however, to ask for answers and solutions. It helps me to easily gain awareness of things that I would like to know or experience. I have been quite amazed to discover that it is even possible to influence the weather on occasions. You can actually use this step to request anything—it's really only limited by one's imagination. It's also fascinating to utilize it in a more *playful* way if you enjoy delightful surprises. Just for fun, make the following request in **Step #4**, and see what happens!

> • *Thank you for providing all the wonderful things that continue to light up my life. I love to receive spontaneous gifts that take me by surprise. I especially appreciate unexpected income that arrives at just the perfect time! When I look forward to good things coming my way, I feel like declaring my own holiday! Thanks again for always coming up with new and exciting ways to make my heart sing!*

Now that you clearly understand this last step, you finally have the complete 15-Minute Miracle formula, which empowers you to deliberately attract more of what you truly desire in life! To make this process extremely quick and easy, I have included an example of a completed 15-Minute Miracle form on page 77. If you desire to obtain a generous supply of full-sized (8 ½" x 11") blank forms, you will want to order the new, expanded edition of My Miracle Manifestation Manual™. This handy workbook serves as your **Personal Miracle Journal** as well as your **Daily Diary** and **Calendar**. It has everything you need to do this process for thirty-one days, plus several other intriguing exercises to help you obtain positive results beyond your wildest expectations. It's the perfect companion to this book, and it's loaded with lots of inspiring examples for you to emulate. (For further information, see pages 137 and 146.)

Give yourself permission to just *play* with these ideas. There's really nothing more important than discovering what makes you happy. If you only invest 15 minutes a day doing the following exercise, you are sure to experience results that most people will only be able to describe as Miracles (for lack of a better way to explain them)! While some like to do their 15-Minute Miracle first thing in the morning, others prefer to do it shortly before they go to bed at night. It doesn't really matter when you choose to do it—the main thing is that you **just do it**! Simply have *fun* with all of this, and the rest will take care of itself! Make a game out of it as you write down what you want—then just spend the rest of the day shopping for "happy coincidences." The more playful you are, the better this works! Be sure to visualize and daydream often, because your dreams are previews of the coming attractions in your life.

 **Secret**

…knowledge lying behind
ordinary comprehension and
known only by very few. The discovery
of *The Seven Secrets of Success* may be
the *key* to achieving your fondest
dreams and desires.

The **Seven Secrets** of Success

Typically, only 3% of the population take the time to commit their goals to paper, but 95% (**a full 95%**) of those who write them down, consistently achieve them! You can greatly *accelerate* the rate at which The 15-Minute Miracle process works for you by paying very close attention to the following suggestions.

1. **Claim 15 minutes a day to just ponder your dreams and desires**. Find a comfortable spot that allows you to enjoy complete privacy. Just 15 minutes of focusing upon what you would l♥ve to experience will very likely save you countless hours of running around in circles. Always start by acknowledging everything for which you are *already* grateful. This is the *key* that opens the door to attracting that which meets or exceeds your wildest expectations. This is the most significant step in the entire process, because it sets the stage for your successful deliberate creation.

2. **Write down the very first thoughts that come into your mind**. If you want to effectively communicate with IT (your Invisible Teacher or your InTuition), simply ask a question (such as, "How would I l♥ve to *feel* today?") Next, *listen* in your mind for that inner voice that clearly whispers (or shouts) the perfect answer. You possess an amazing inner guidance system. When you feel inspired, uplifted, or encouraged (positive emotion), you'll *know* you're on the right track. Learn to *trust* your feelings (even if they do not make perfect sense to you right away). Before long, you will see evidence of how wise you were to follow your heart and your *hunches*.

3. **Be sure to a-l-w-a-y-s phrase your statements from a totally positive perspective**. If your Statements of Desire are *purely positive,* you will get *purely positive* results. In other words, only focus upon *one* thing—that which you want to attract into your life. Below is a good example of a statement that evokes a wonderful sense of well-being.

> *It's fun to feel **exhilarated** and **excited** about achieving my goals in life.*

This statement will definitely invite positive results, because you are focused exclusively upon feeling *exhilarated* and *excited*. If, however, you were to say, "Today, I *desperately* want to feel free of *depression*, so I won't feel so *devastated*," you will undoubtedly attract a very *undesirable* outcome—more desperation, depression, and devastation. If you desire to feel *uplifted* and in charge of your life, all you have to do is imagine how wonderful it would feel to be exhilarated and self-confident. ✦ Life can only bring you that which you give your attention to, so focus *only* upon things that truly delight you!

Whatever you push away, you get more of! If you focus upon what you want to get rid of, you will only attract *more* of what you *don't* want. When you ask to "lose" something (like weight), just know that you are asking to become a "loser!" Furthermore, if your request is a combination of a positive *and* a negative statement, such as "I would l♥ve to feel *good,* because I'm sick and tired of feeling *bad,*" one cancels out the other. This results in no change for you!

4. **Expand your statements by describing the benefits of achieving each goal**. Be artistic—paint beautiful and descriptive word pictures to express how you *feel* as you imagine that your requests have already granted. Just have fun as you follow each statement with words like…

    "When I_____, then I_____, which enables me to _____.

    > *I now choose to invite people and events into my life that tickle my funny bone.* **When I** *just let go and laugh uncontrollably,* **then I** *feel a wonderful sense of release and exhilaration,* **which enables me to** *enjoy my day, regardless of circumstances!*

This added step is fun to do, and it works like magic! It speeds up your ability to attract extraordinary results, because it causes you to stay focused upon the object of your desires. Your whole body chemistry responds to your positive anticipation in a way that makes you feel absolutely wonderful! This definitely adds to the quality of your health, because it boosts your immune system. Soon, you are bound to recognize the correlation between what you *think* and what you *experience*. The day you make this connection is the day you can take charge of your life and attract the fulfillment of your dreams and desires with incredible ease!

5. **It's fun and effective to add tag lines to your requests** such as: "easily and effortlessly," "this or something greater," "in just the perfect time," "in ways that totally delight me," "in the highest and best good of all concerned," "for things known and unknown," "from now on," "that meets or exceeds my wildest expectations," etc. (see example).

> *I now choose to playfully attract and create unexpected income* **easily and effortlessly, in just the perfect time, in ways that totally delight me**. *When I invite unlimited abundance* **that meets or exceeds my wildest expectations**, *I feel like an elated child who knows that all things are truly possible, which enables me to experience sustained joy. I look forward to* **this or something greater from now on**!

6. **Engage the magical principles of "Positive Expectancy"**—just *believe* in your heart that your wishes have *already* been granted (even though physical evidence may not yet be apparent). This is an extremely powerful ingredient in your recipe of deliberate creation. To enable your dreams and desires to be realized with incredible ease, just remember…all things are possible for those who *believe*.

7. **Now for the greatest secret of all**! If you really want to attract actual ✴Miracles into your life in the quickest and easiest way possible, all you have to do is…1) *identify* your desires…2) *invite* them into your life by *asking* for them…3) have *faith* that they will be made manifest…4) then be *willing* to *release* your *attachment* to the outcome. Be **willing** to **release** your **attachment** to the outcome—more simply stated…

"Let go and let ✴God."

Just *decide* what you want, and call it forth by *basking* in how wonderful it would *feel* to experience it. Focus only upon that which makes you *smile, laugh,* and feel fully *connected* to ✳Life—those feelings that cause the floodgates of *abundance* and the doors of *opportunity* to fly wide open for you! As strange as this may seem, this is how you can create incredibly positive results for yourself.

Your job is to know what you want! ✳**Life's job is to attend to all the details** (who, when, why, where, and how). Therefore, just focus upon that which you desire, then leave the rest to the discretion of the same magnificent ✳Power that creates worlds. Since you are very likely to *get* whatever you *ask* for, be sure to invite it to come to you in a way that is in harmony with your well-being. For instance, request that things come to you in just the perfect time and in ways that totally delight you. Otherwise, you may get what you want, but not in the appropriate time or in a way that is convenient. As Walt Disney often said to those who longed to turn their ideas into physical realities,

*"If you can **Dream** it, you can **Do** it!"*

Right about now, you may be wondering whether it is beneficial to ask for things more than once. Technically, it's only necessary to ask *once,* but it's perfectly okay to *daydream* and *visualize* yourself being, doing, or having whatever you have requested in a way that makes you feel *happy* just to think about it. In fact, *imagining* a positive outcome will definitely attract desired results more quickly. If, however, you ask with a desperate sense of *longing*, you actually sabotage yourself, because you are so focused upon "not having." Be sure to stay focused upon that which delights you, and remember…

Your **Dreams** *are* ✳**Miracles** *just waiting to* **Happen**!

At last, you are ready to do 𝕿𝖍𝖊 15-𝕸𝖎𝖓𝖚𝖙𝖊 ✳𝕸𝖎𝖗𝖆𝖈𝖑𝖊 process in its entirety. The most important thing for you to do now is simply to *relax* and *enjoy* yourself. Give yourself *permission* to have fun with all of this! *Allow* your thoughts and words to flow freely, and you will be absolutely amazed at how good you will begin to feel right away. This could very well be the ✳Miracle you have been looking for—it could be the "missing piece" in your puzzle of life! You will soon be able to easily go from wherever you are now to wherever you truly prefer to be!

✳Miracles
are truly **Yours**
just for the "**Basking**!"

...basking in the realization that
All Things Really *Are* Possible!

If you will invest just **15 Minutes a Day** for the next **21 Days**
filling out your personal 15-Minute ✳Miracle forms,
you will discover for yourself how you can easily
attract actual ✳ *Miracles & Incredible Coincidences*
into your own life on a regular and
predictable basis!

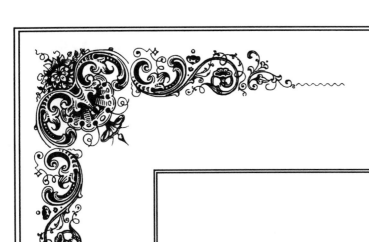

✳ 15 Minutes

…a quarter of an hour
or **1/96ᵗʰ of a day**. There are
exactly 1,440 minutes in each day.
In only 15 minutes a day, you can easily
transform fear into l♥ve, worry into
well-being, and scarcity into
unlimited abundance!

My 15-Minute ✦ Miracle™

> What I *fill* my mind with, my life is *full* of!

Today, (Date) _____ *Saturday, February 7, 1998* _____ , *is a* **Clean Slate** *for me to enjoy.*

Today, I really **Appreciate**…, because it enables and/or inspires me to…*(emphasize benefits)*

- *Today, I really* **Appreciate** *the unconditional love and support that I feel from my husband,* because it inspires me to *support all of his dreams in the same open and loving way!*

- *Today, I really* **Appreciate** *the gift of The 15-Minute Miracle,* because it enables me to *feel in perfect balance and harmony with all that is.*

I love to **Feel**…When I…, then I…, which enables me to…*(emphasize benefits)*

- *I love to* **Feel** *a sense of having all the time in the world to do whatever I desire at my own pace and in my own way.* When I *feel I have time to spare,* then I *am able to savor each moment as it comes,* which enables me to *experience a tremendous sense of well-being. Ah-h-h—life is good!*

I now **Choose** *to…(do whatever delights me!)* When I…, then I…, which enables me to…*(emphasize benefits)*

- *I now* **Choose** *to accomplish all that I set out to do easily and effortlessly.* When I *finish whatever I start,* then I *feel really good about myself,* which enables me to *do even more. I eagerly look forward to this outcome or something greater.*

- *I now* **Choose** *to have an exceptionally fun-filled day with lots of pleasant surprises!* When I *look forward to positive possibilities and delightful situations,* then I *feel extremely vital and exhilarated,* which enables me to *remember how grateful I am to be alive.*

Note: Determine how much (or how little) to write each day by how you feel. Write down whatever flows easily through your awareness until you feel complete with it. It's really quite easy—all you have to do is…1) focus upon what makes your heart sing, and…2) just have fun as you play with this process.

I now choose to **Invite Assistance** *from* ✴ *The L♥ving Power that Created All That Is.*
Thank you,_____God_____, for always being here for me. I so appreciate when all things come to me in just the perfect time in ways that totally delight me. I l♥ve knowing that opportunities are limitless and that all is really well. **Thank you for your support in providing the following things that I perceive to be beyond my *own* ability to achieve:**

> *I look forward to discovering the most delightful way to do what I love for a living. I particularly enjoy uplifting and inspiring others, because it fills my heart with inexplicable joy. I want to embrace my work with the kind of passion that creates so much momentum that it takes on a life of its own and allows me to ignite with delight. Most of all, I prefer to remain in balance with the Universe, in rhythm with Life, and in harmony with Your love. Thank you for always granting my requests.*

Today, I am willing to **Release and Let Go** *of…the belief that I have to do everything myself in order to be satisfied with the results.*
I now release all issues (*known and unknown*) that no longer serve me in a positive way, which enables me to…*clear my mind, clarify my thinking, and claim my spirit! That feels so-o-o good.*

I now **Give Myself Permission** *to…,* which enables me to…*(emphasize benefits) relax in a hot bath and read a good book for at least a half hour, which enables me to rest my body and renew my energy. I look forward to enjoying this time out to just "be."*

Desirable Things *to have…*

- *a Seagull "Grand" guitar*
- *a surprise gift that delights me*
- *an HP Laser Jet 6L printer*

Delightful Situations *to attract…*

- *a well-organized work environment*
- *demonstration of unexpected income*
- *favorable outcome to the IRS audit*

Results: (✴ *Miracle-like events that have happened to me in response to my previous requests!*)

- *I received unexpected income of $267 today (Discover Card bonus).*
- *Ron surprised me with the HP Laser Jet 6L printer that I asked for.*
- *The IRS audit is over and resulted in a huge credit in our favor!*

Note: The things and events you record here could be a reflection of things you have asked for in the past.

With heartfelt thanks, **I am Open** *to receive all of the above!* ♨

Signed… *Jacquelyn Aldana*   Date… *February 7, 1998*

Copyright © 1995 by Jacquelyn Aldana ✴ *S.o.L.* **1-888-In The Flow** (that's **1-888-468-4335**)

78

Because this simple formula is based upon ageless universal laws that are immutable and absolute, **there's no way it cannot work for you!** It has the potential to work for absolutely *anyone* who has a sincere desire to be happy. If you just focus all of your attention upon that which you desire to experience,

you can **deliberately attract and create** *whatever you* **choose** *in life!*

Just do it every day for the next three weeks, and prove it to yourself. Whatever you can do for **twenty-one consecutive days**, you can easily do for the rest of your life. By then it becomes a *way* of life. Perhaps you are saying to yourself, "**Do I need to do this every single day?**" Absolutely not! I don't do it every day myself—only on the days that I want to feel *happy, healthy, inspired, encouraged, motivated*, and *capable* of choosing what happens to me in life! On the days I neglect to do it, I definitely notice a dramatic difference!

For best results, **write down your dreams and desires** and vividly *imagine* how wonderful things *could* be (writing has proven to be the most effective method of attracting desired results). As I mentioned in The Seven Secrets of Success on page 71, **you have a 95% chance of achieving your goals** by merely writing them down on paper! When you take the time to write them on paper (or record them on tape), ✴Life has no choice but to respond to you in a positive way! Just casually *thinking* about what you want is not nearly as effective, because you have over 60,000 thoughts competing for your attention every day. Suggestion: "**Write 'em and reap!**"

It's fun to keep track of your experiences on your 15-Minute ✴Miracle forms. Take a few minutes at the end of your day to make a note of all the marvels, ✴Miracles, and incredible coincidences that just *magically* showed up in your life. Notice the "Results" section on the back of the example form on page 78. This provides you with your own **Personal ✴Miracle Journal**, which shows you what you have been attracting and creating on a daily basis. This enables you to easily make the connection between what you *think about* and what you actually *bring about*. It's extremely revealing! Once you realize how capable and powerful you really are, you are bound to enjoy life more than ever before. If you're like most of us, you'll begin to wonder how you ever made it through life this far without knowing about The 15-Minute ✴Miracle!

We don't stop

playing because we get **Old**.

We get old, because we

stop **Playing**!

source unknown

Positive Perceptions and Playful Possibilities

So far, you have been reading about how important it is to always stay "positively focused." Although this is definitely the easiest way to attract that which you desire, most of us are all too aware of what we *don't* want in life! It's perfectly okay to briefly (and I mean *briefly*) acknowledge the things that make you feel *bad,* because it enables you to clearly identify what makes you feel *better.* Out of what you *don't* want in life (contrast) erupts a poignant awareness of what you *do* want (desire). This is a very *good* thing!

Because contrast allows us to acknowledge the differences in things, it invites us to make choices based upon our preferences. Fortunately, it's not always related to things that we perceive as "bad." If everything were the same color, all foods tasted the same, and everybody looked exactly alike, there would be very little stimulation and exhilaration in life for any of us. While it's fun to recognize the similarities in life, it's also beneficial to appreciate and celebrate the differences (contrast). Diversity is what makes life so interesting—it provides variety…and variety is truly the *spice* of life.

On the pages that follow are a variety of examples to give you an idea of how to counter your negative feelings with positive thoughts. Notice how brief the Statements of Contrast are, compared to the Statements of Desire. The less time you spend observing what you *don't* want, and the more time you spend envisioning what you *do* want, the more successful you will be at deliberately attracting the fulfillment of your desires. These examples will assist you in phrasing your requests in a way that makes you feel good in a hurry. Although I tend to embellish my own writing by painting lots of colorful word pictures, please know that it is equally as effective to make your statements very brief and to the point. It is not the number of words or even the words themselves that are so important—it's the feeling *behind* the words that creates the point of attraction, which in turn determines your destiny.

Below are several of my favorite Statements of Desire that have worked very well for me. *Your* best results will come from using words that evoke strong, positive feelings within *you*. Your creative ideas serve to attract *more* of whatever you are focused upon. Please notice that I have added a sentence, starting with the words "I AM," near the end of each Statement of Desire. Although this part of the process is considered optional, it definitely adds an affirmative punch to your requests. If it feels good to you, go ahead and use it!

♥**If I am thinking,** *"I just don't know what I want,"* **I simply write…**

I now *choose* to discover what really makes my heart sing in a way that totally delights me. When I have a clear picture of what I really want to be, do, or have, I can easily attract it into my life experience. It's fun to clearly focus my attention upon my dreams until they magically *ignite* into physical realities. I feel so empowered to be able to deliberately attract and create whatever my heart desires through the power of my intention. The best part is that it's all so quick and easy. Today, **I AM** an expression of positive anticipation as I eagerly look forward to the magnificent unfolding of ✶Life's intriguing surprises.

♥**If I am thinking,** *"I wish I didn't worry so much about everything,"* **I simply write…**

I now *choose* to invite a sense of well-being and a strong inner knowing that I am equal to any challenge that ✶Life may offer me for the purpose of my expanded awareness. When I feel confident and balanced, I approach things from a more positive

82

perspective, which enables me to attract desired results easily and effortlessly. It feels so good to be "in charge" of my life. Today, **I AM** a glowing reflection of well-being as I acknowledge the abundant evidence that life is fun and all is well.

♥**If I am thinking**, *"I feel so frustrated, insecure, and inadequate,"* **I simply write**...

It's extremely empowering to feel a strong sense of self-appreciation, self-confidence, and self-acceptance. When I feel l♥vable and capable, I feel good about myself, which enables me to easily attract more positive people and experiences into my life. I now choose to release and let go of all things, both known and unknown, that no longer serve me in a positive way. Today, **I AM** an enlightened expression of self-realization as I fondly remember the positive things that others have said about me in the past.

♥**If I am thinking**, *"I'm sick and tired of feeling so sick and tired,"* **I simply write**...

I now *choose* to discover an easy way by which to enjoy radiant health from now on. I l♥ve being able to naturally exude abundant energy. When I feel mentally sharp and physically strong, I view life with an extraordinary sense of optimism, which automatically attracts *more* things for me to appreciate. As I find additional things to appreciate, I feel better and have more energy. Today, **I AM** a radiant expression of wellness as I acknowledge and appreciate the aspects of my body that operate with total precision.

♥**If I am thinking**, *"If only I didn't have to struggle to fall asleep at night,"* **I simply write**...

I am so lucky to be able to relax completely when I lie down to rest. It feels so good to be able to drift off naturally into a deep, peaceful sleep at night. It's wonderful to have pleasant dreams and wake up feeling totally refreshed in the morning. When I enjoy a good night's sleep, I'm inspired to appreciate life, which enables me to enjoy my day. Today, **I AM** completely renewed as I recall times in the past when I fell asleep easily and effortlessly.

♥ **If I am thinking**, *"I'm out of work, and I can't find a decent job,"* **I simply write**…

I now *choose* to invite an awareness into my life that allows me to easily recognize my perfect vocational opportunity. When I keep myself open to all positive possibilities, I am often surprised with delightful situations as they just *magically* unfold. I look forward to finding my ideal job in just the perfect time in ways that invite my confidence to soar. All of this enables me to keep focused upon an exciting new adventure that I have yet to discover. Today, **I AM** a pure, positive expression of enthusiasm, because I know there are several outstanding employers actively looking for someone with my skills, experience, and integrity. In fact, they are probably actively searching for me right now!

♥ **If I am thinking** *"I dread having confrontations with _____,"* **I simply write**…

I now *choose* to invite harmony, warmth, and understanding into my relationship with _____. When I merely appreciate his (her) positive qualities, I automatically begin to feel better, and he (she) seems to respond to me in a much more positive way. This, in turn, enables me to feel much more encouraged, uplifted, and validated. As I release *my* need to judge and control the actions of others, others are then inspired to release *their* need to judge and control me. Releasing and letting go of judgment is one of the most freeing and empowering things I have ever experienced! Today, **I AM** totally free and extremely exhilarated as I release the temptation to judge and control _____.

♥ **If I am thinking**, *"I'm tired of feeling so down and discouraged,"* **I simply write**…

I now *choose* to invite a sense of joy and exhilaration into my life from now on. When I feel happy, I have abundant energy and enthusiasm, which enables me to be, do, or have whatever delights me! I l♥ve that feeling of being connected to ✴ Life, because it reminds me that all is really well. The quickest way for me to feel good is to find things to appreciate and admire. I automatically feel inspired and encouraged when I recall the things for which I am truly grateful. Today, **I AM** uplifted as I ponder the idea of discovering many new things for which to give thanks.

♥**If I am thinking**, *"I sure wish I had someone 'special' in my life,"* **I simply write**…

I now *choose* to extend a warm invitation to my ideal mate to come into my life in just the perfect time, in a way that totally delights me. I l♥ve the kind of relationship that allows us to bring out the best in one another. I prefer a thoughtful, gentle person with a great sense of humor, who is easy to get along with and enchanting to be with. I look forward to experiencing the magic of a special connection that is so harmonious that words cannot even begin to describe how wonderful it feels. When I merely ponder this "perfect partnership," I experience a wonderful sense of well-being and positive anticipation about life, which enables me to easily express all of the same qualities that I am seeking in my mate. Today, **I AM** a l♥ving expression of joy, exhilaration, and spontaneity as I offer my heart to my best friend whom I have yet to meet.

♥**If I am thinking**, *"I hate struggling to just make ends meet,"* **I simply write**…

I now *choose* to find an easy and entertaining way to create wealth. Just as I know that I have access to plenty of air to breathe, water to drink, and thoughts to think, I remember that I can claim as much happiness and prosperity as I am willing to *believe* I deserve. When I give myself *permission* to fill my own cup, then I am able to share all that I have with others, which enables me to be of greater value to myself and everyone else. Today, **I AM** a stellar expression of affluence as I am now *willing* to accept my divine inheritance. Starting today, I am completely open to receive unexpected income from sources I have yet to discover.

♥**If I am thinking**, *"I feel awful about always putting things off,"* **I simply write**…

I now *choose* to find simple and creative ways to accomplish things that I have had great resistance to even starting (up until now). I "want to want" to start and finish my projects in ways that are fun, interesting, and entertaining. When I accomplish what I set out to do, I feel so good about myself. The positive momentum naturally enables me to do even *more* with amazing ease. I appreciate the wonderful peace of mind that I experience when there is order in my life. Today, **I AM** an outstanding expression of achievement as I discover the quickest and most enjoyable ways by which to accomplish my goals.

85

♥**If I am thinking,** *"I wish I could get rid of the pain in my body,"* **I simply write**…

It feels so good to enjoy soothing comfort and abundant flexibility in my body. Just contemplating radiant health allows me to feel better. When I feel good physically, I enjoy more energy, which enables me to savor each precious moment as it gracefully unfolds. Although I do not consciously know the details of achieving my health-related goals, I *do* know that I shall settle for nothing less than what I really desire to experience. Since countless others have successfully regained their wellness, **I know that I can do it too**! Today, **I AM** a joyous expression of gratitude as I appreciate all of the aspects of my physical body that continue to serve me well. I am grateful for the degree of comfort that I *already* have and look forward to even *more* vitality with each day that passes.

For some *additional* examples of Statements of Desire, you may refer to 𝓜𝓎 ✝ 𝓜𝓲𝓻𝓪𝓬𝓵𝓮 𝓜𝓪𝓷𝓲𝓯𝓮𝓼𝓽𝓪𝓽𝓲𝓸𝓷 𝓜𝓪𝓷𝓾𝓪𝓵™ which is a perfect companion to *this* book (see description on page 138). There are lots of good ideas in the section entitled…

"Positive Possibilities for You to Ponder and Appreciate."

I hear, **I Forget**
I see, **I Remember**
I do, **I Understand**

Moshe Feldenkrais

Part 5

- The ✦ Secret Behind The 15-Minute ✦ Miracle

- If You Want to Be ✦ Free, Just Learn to ✦ Be

- The Law of ✦ Positive Expectancy

- You Can If You ✦ Think You Can

- If I Only Knew Then What I Know ✦ Now

- Instructions for Living a ✦ Happy Life

"…**Ask**, and it shall be given to you;

Seek, and you shall find;

Knock, and it shall be

opened unto you."

"For everyone who asks, **Receives**;

and he who seeks, **Finds**;

and to him who knocks,

it shall be **Opened**."

(Matthew: 7:7 & 7:8)

or more simply stated…

If you don't **Ask**,
you don't **Get**!

Mahatma Gandhi

The ✳ **Secret** Behind
The 15-Minute ✳ Miracle

"The fool wonders—the wise man asks!"
Benjamin Disraeli

The fascinating *secrets* revealed in this chapter have the potential to transform your life in a very positive way almost *overnight!* If you are like most people, you find it difficult to *ask* anyone for anything. Why do you suppose that is? We actually surveyed a number of individuals to determine what kept them from asking for what they truly wanted in life. This is what they typically told us:

"I don't like criticism."

"It's too much trouble!"

"Maybe I don't deserve it."

"It makes me uncomfortable."

"I would rather do it all myself."

"Someone might think I am ignorant."

"I can't stand the thought of rejection."

"I don't want to be obligated to others."

All this apprehension stems from just plain **fear** and our innate **desire for approval** from others. Many of us are incredibly afraid of the unknown—we find it far too painful to take the risk of being *judged, rejected*, or possibly *criticized* by others. This fear totally immobilizes us and causes us to stay right where we are—even if we *know* we don't really want to be there.

Now that we have examined several reasons why *not* to ask, let's look to see what could happen if we *did* ask:

89

"I could have fun."

"I could get a job."

"I could get a raise."

"I could get new ideas."

"I could simplify my life."

"I could learn something."

"I could save a lot of time."

"I could get what I ask for."

"I could save a lot of money."

"I could increase my income."

"I could get some good advice."

"People may be delighted to help."

"I could obtain valuable information."

"I could meet new and interesting people."

"I could benefit from the experience of others."

When you examine all the benefits of asking, it really becomes something worth considering. The next logical step is to figure out *who* and *how* to ask. For now, I am only going to focus upon a couple of key ideas for you to ponder. To *master* the art of asking, I highly recommend you read **The Aladdin Factor** by Jack Canfield and Mark Victor Hansen (authors of **Chicken Soup for the Soul**). This book will definitely help you find courage and comfort in asking for anything your heart truly desires. Since the *secret* behind The 15-Minute Miracle is learning how to *ask*, it may be well worth your time to become really good at it!

One of the most powerful steps in The 15-Minute Miracle consists of inviting assistance from The Loving Power that Created All That Is. We are actually *asking* the very same Power that created worlds to provide us with that which we desire…and because we are putting our thoughts in writing, we feel obliged to be extremely *clear* about what we *choose* to request. Fortunately, most of us are comfortable calling upon an invisible✢Power greater than ourselves. In fact, this is what we typically *do* when we perceive things to be beyond our *own* ability to achieve —we become inspired to pray. Since our requests are totally private, we have no fear of confrontation, criticism, or personal rejection—after all, who is going to know we even asked?

When you think about what truly makes you happy, your entire mind (conscious, subconscious, and superconscious) is clearly focused upon what you *intend* to attract. Like all universal laws, The Law of Magnetic Attraction is totally impersonal. It operates exactly the same way for everyone—**there are absolutely no exceptions**! It has **no choice** but to bring you those things that are in harmony with your thoughts and feelings. This is why you are likely to experience *happy coincidences* on a pretty regular basis when you focus upon things that delight you. Although this intriguing process is extremely *simple,* it is also incredibly *powerful!* The 15-Minute✢Miracle gives a whole new and expanded meaning to the statement, "Wonders never cease." There is no way this process can fail to work for you if you just apply the basic principles!

Have you ever been in the predicament of knowing what you *don't* want, yet not knowing what you *do* want? If so, you'll be glad to know that there is a very simple solution to this conundrum. Go to *Fantasy Island* in the playground of your imagination… take a deep breath…and ask yourself this question:

*"If all things were **ideal**, how would I **feel**?"*

Imagine you had all the time in the world, unlimited financial resources, and responsibility only for yourself. You will be *amazed* at how you feel when you just let your imagination run wild. Just notice how *excited* and *exhilarated* you become when you contemplate all the limitless possibilities—go ahead and write down everything you can think of. This usually clarifies, in your own mind, what you honestly want out of life. In the moment you begin to imagine how wonderful things *can* be, you begin to attract wonderful results! This is the first and most important step in the process of deliberate creation. Once you feel that "connectedness with✢Life," you'll know things are changing for the better.

The next idea to be offered is extremely fun, and it definitely has the potential to *supercharge* your life—in fact, this idea alone may be worth the price of this book! It is appropriately referred to as "**The Advice Call**" and is one of the most extraordinary concepts I have ever come across. Allow me to give you an example of how I used this amazing door-opening technique when I needed to find a way to make a major change in my employment.

About 20 years ago, I felt as though I were in a rut with regard to my job. I knew I didn't like being there, yet I had no idea where I wanted to go. Because I had no solutions of my own, I ended up investing thousands of dollars to retain the services of an outstanding executive guidance firm. This ultimately led to a most enlightening discovery!

After I ascertained which career possibilities offered me the greatest sense of exhilaration, I researched to find out who were among the most successful in those areas of expertise. I then made a point to find out as much as I could about their achievements. I even wrote letters congratulating them on their impressive accomplishments and politely asked for an appointment. Knowing they were very busy, I always offered to take them out to lunch. I began by telling them how much I admired them as positive role models, and then I went on to say..."I plan to dedicate myself to becoming a highly successful _____, and I am seeking expert advice from positive role models who are already very successful. That's why I specifically chose to talk to you, _____."

The results were absolutely astounding! Not only did they offer me valuable inside information, but they often offered me a job as well. If they couldn't help me personally, they got on the phone and called everyone they knew who *could* help. They even took the time to set up more appointments for me. Everywhere I went, I received tremendous help and support from people I had never even met before. My self-worth and self-esteem just skyrocketed. As I began to consciously appreciate my *own* attributes, others treated me as though I were exceptional—as though I really had something of enormous value to offer. When I want to move forward in *any* area of my life and have a lot of fun doing it, I just make one advice call after the other. It's not only a lot of fun, but it's also extremely rewarding.

*You'll be absolutely **amazed** at the results!*

The whole purpose of telling you this story is to emphasize the value of *asking* for advice and assistance. Most people are absolutely thrilled when asked for their opinion on something. They consider it a compliment that you are interested in their point of view, and they usually have a sincere desire to be of service to you.

Although this is optional, you might enjoy making a "practice" advice call (just for fun), so you can see how easy it is. Pretend you are a reporter and that you are writing a story to help your readers discover the most effective way to become self-employed. Now find the most extraordinary role model you can—a very successful entrepreneur! Next, write this person a letter explaining who you are and that you have a burning desire to also become self-employed. Promise to take only 5 to15 minutes to ask just three questions that will very likely make an enormous positive difference in your life. It's advisable to call your prospect and offer to take him (her) out for lunch if you desire more than a few minutes of his (her) time. Make up a list of questions that will help your interviewee give you the information you desire.

After completing your advice call, it really helps to express appreciation and send a thank-you note within 24 hours. **Most importantly, release all attachment to the outcome!** Just have fun with this playful process! This is truly one of the most delightful and comfortable ways to develop an enormous amount of self-confidence and enthusiasm! Throw all caution to the wind and just do it! The only thing you really have to lose is your fear of asking for assistance.

Go for it! 👍

✦ Unconditional L♥ve

...total *acceptance*, not
limited in any way by conditions
or qualifications. ✦ God l♥ves each one
of us unconditionally. The energy that sur-
rounds unconditional l♥ve is the same
precious energy that created our
own magnificent ✦ Universe!

94

If You Want to **Be ✳ Free**
Just **Learn to ✳ Be**

"Live and let live."

Wouldn't it be marvelous if other people would accept you just the way you are? Wouldn't it be wonderful to know that you are l♥ved (and not judged in any way) as you joyfully *choose* your life experiences? Although you may not always meet with the approval of everyone, there is an amazingly simple way to favorably influence others to accept you *more* unconditionally than they do now. **Here is the secret:** Whenever you observe another person (regardless of who it is), make a point to say to yourself as you go through your day…

> "**I am** *that which* **I am**, *and I am* **willing** *to*
> **allow** *all others to* **be** *that which* **they are**."

Jerry and Esther Hicks of *Abraham Speaks*

This instantly relieves you of the need to judge or control the actions of others. This is the *key* to giving and receiving unconditional l♥ve. This non-judgmental expression of affection is best demonstrated by our animal friends (that's why my highest aspiration is to become the awesome person my dog *thinks* I am)! Let's take *your* pet for example —have you ever noticed that your _____ (dog, cat, etc.) totally adores you no matter…

what you **do**, *how you* **look**, *or how you* **act**?

The reason most people are so devoted to their animals is because their loyal companions never judge them. Animals instinctively l♥ve their human friends no matter what. They are extraordinary role models. Even though your adorable furry friend may have a little accident on the rug or might totally destroy something of yours that is quite valuable, you find yourself rationalizing your little darling's behavior. Because

95

you truly adore your bel♥ved pet, you overlook such things (the eyes of l♥ve can only see perfection and potential). This is really unconditional l♥ve in its purest form—

l♥ving *another* **regardless** *of conditions!*

When you begin to express these warm feelings toward the rest of your human family, you will find that they (just like your l♥ving animal buddies) will be much more inclined to accept you just the way you are. The bottom line is this—when you release *your* need to judge and control others, then others will be more inclined to release *their* need to judge and control you. I think you'll agree that it feels much better to be "in l♥ve" than to be "in control!"

The truest test of l♥ving unconditionally is to l♥ve others even when they display less than unconditional l♥ve toward you. Even if others persist in judging you, just continue to *allow* them to think and believe as they choose. They are undoubtedly doing the very best they can with their current level of understanding of how life works. Please know that if they **could** do better, they certainly **would** do better, and…

if **you** *could do better,* **you** *would do better too!*

We are all at different stages of awareness as we move through our lives. As long as you do *your* part, however, you will experience a sense of well-being that allows you to be happy in *spite* of conditions. Simply **allow others to be who they are**. It is also important to realize that this is not the same as merely *tolerating* them. When you are *allowing,* you feel a comforting sense of harmony and contentment. When you merely *tolerate* someone's behavior, you will surely feel negative emotion—you will inadvertently stop the flow of pure, positive energy that would otherwise flow freely to you. All you have to do is notice how you *feel,* and you will *know* if you are allowing or just tolerating.

Unconditional l♥ve may not be so easy to practice at first; however, the benefits are well worth your effort to become good at it. Have you noticed that when others l♥ve us unconditionally, **they naturally bring out the best in us?** We become eager to emulate them—we want to pass along the kindness that *we* received. When we simply accept others, *regardless* of conditions, they tend to respond to us in a much kinder manner as well. Just ponder this idea for a while, and see how it *feels* to you.

Most authorities agree that blame, guilt, jealousy, and resentment actually keep us from realizing our goals in life—these negative emotions also seriously jeopardize our health. We can relieve ourselves of these stressful feelings by using the simple procedure outlined below. Although it is similar to "forgiveness," *this* technique enables us to release our resentments toward others in a way that invites us to let go of *our* attachment to the issue. You'll most likely feel 1,000 pounds lighter as you engage in this self-empowering process. The essence of this idea originated from Gail Montgomery, a very l♥ving and talented psychotherapist from Arkansas.

> **"I am willing to release** *the blame that surrounds any resentfulness I am feeling, and* **I agree to allow** *whoever* **caused** *my resentments to carry these negative feelings, if they belong to him (her)! May all things that no longer serve me in a positive way be magically transformed into the pure, positive energy of unconditional l♥ve."*

This implies that **justice is somehow being served**, which allows most people to feel better right away. As you embrace the principles of 𝕿𝖍𝖊 15-𝕸inute 🕇 𝕸iracle, however, you will probably graduate to the method outlined in the next example. In the meantime, please feel free to use the previous technique as a "bridge," until you no longer feel the need for it.

> **"I am willing to release and let go** *of my need to blame others for undesirable conditions in my life.* **I now choose to take full responsibility** *for creating my own sense of worth and well-being, because I finally realize that* **I am the cause of my life experiences** *(both good and bad). From now on,* **I choose** *to invite a warm sense of harmony and balance into my life.* **I fully intend** *to find joy and delight in every moment as it magically unfolds.*

Until we release and let go of the past, we will never be truly free to enjoy the present moment, and "The Present" is all we really have! It's helpful to remember this catchy little saying…

The past is **History***, the future is a* **Mystery***,*
but today is a **Gift***. That's why it's called "***The Present***."*

97

✳ Positive Expectancy

...looking forward to
something with a delightful
sense of anticipation. It implies a high
degree of certainty and usually involves
preparing or envisioning things
that contribute to a sense of
joy and well-being.

The Law of
✧ Positive Expectancy

"Expect a ✝ Miracle"

Dan Wakefield

"…All things for which you pray and ask,
believe *that you have received them,*
and they shall be granted you."

(Mark 11:24)

Since recorded history, healers and physicians have successfully utilized the placebo effect, because it has produced amazing results. It works because…

the **body** *is healed by the* **mind** *(not the other way around)!*

Placebos are simply neutral preparations (sugar pills) that are given in order to comfort patients who believe they are ill or deficient in some way. It is interesting to note that the literal Latin translation of the word "placebo" is "**I shall please!**" When the mind really *believes* that a pill or procedure will provide a cure, the body immediately *responds* by producing the necessary chemicals, hormones, and drugs to heal itself. When you begin to grasp the significance of this idea, you are better able to deliberately create favorable circumstances in your life.

There is a humorous example of this phenomenon demonstrated by a woman who had insomnia for a couple of weeks. She had such great difficulty sleeping that she had to obtain a prescription from her doctor for sleeping pills. That night she took two pills and slept like a baby. She was puzzled, however, when she awoke to find the two pills still lying on the table next to her bed. Then she suddenly remembered that she had promised to sew *two buttons* on her husband's shirt and noticed that **both buttons were missing from her nightstand** (talk about The Law of Positive Expectancy)!

99

*"But how can I **believe** in that which I've not yet seen?"*

The answer lies in simply *trusting* that the laws of the Universe *do* work and that they *will* work for you. Dr. Wayne Dyer wrote a wonderful book appropriately entitled ***You'll See It When You Believe It*** that elaborates upon the answer to this question. If you believe in The Law of Gravity and The Law of Magnetic Attraction, you can be 100% sure that...

The 15-Minute Miracle
will work for you!

Most of us cannot explain (in technical terms) how electricity works, yet we use it nearly every day of our lives. We expect that when we plug in a lamp and turn it on, that we shall have light. The 15-Minute Miracle is a lot like electricity. You do not need to know how it works (in a technical sense); however, you can plug into it and *use* it as often as you like. The best part is that this magical process has been divinely designed to consistently work in *your* favor—all you have to do is simply follow the easy-to-apply principles.

There is actually **no way it can't work for you**!

It's really amazing! It doesn't seem to matter whether you understand it or even believe in it—it seems to work anyway! It works best, however, when you do the process as outlined in this book, then **completely release your attachment to the outcome**. This is definitely the *key* to manifesting Miracles in your life. I personally experience the most favorable results when I just have fun and play with this process. When I deeply *long* for something, I unavoidably attract more lack and limitation into my life. This is because I am so focused upon what I *don't* have. When I simply bask in the possibilities of how things *could* be if all things were ideal, then I consistently get results that amaze and delight me. The best news is that **you can do the same thing**! If you want to gain even further benefit, share some of these inspiring ideas with others. The more you explain it to another person, the better you will understand it yourself.

You **Can** If You  **Think** You **Can**!

If you **think** you are beaten, you are
If you **think** you dare not, you don't
If you like to win, but you **think** you can't
It's almost certain you won't

If you **think** you'll lose, you've lost
For out in the world we find
Success begins with a person's will
It's all in the state of mind

If you **think** you are outclassed, you are
You've got to **think** high to rise
You've got to be sure of yourself before
You ever can win the prize

Life's triumphs don't always go
To the stronger or faster man
But sooner or later the man who wins
Is the man who **thinks** he can

Quoted from *The Spice of Life* by Dian Ritter

If you don't

have l♥ve for ✴**Yourself**,

you can't be l♥ving

to ✴**Others**.

Dr. Wayne Dyer

If I Only Knew **Then** What I Know ✴ **Now**

Recently, while doing some spring cleaning and organizing my files, I happened to find something I never even realized I had. I was so thrilled to discover this unexpected gift, as it offered me a sweet bouquet of *fresh possibilities* to consider. "What was this intriguing and delightful treasure?" you ask. It was a warm letter of welcome from ✴ *The L♥ving Power that Created All That Is*, entitled…

Instructions for Living a ✴ Happy Life.

I seem to have learned my lessons of life the hard way—it took me quite a while to figure things out. I probably could have saved a lot of time and trouble if only I had read these instructions much earlier. Until I embraced these l♥ving words of wisdom, I was thoroughly convinced it was socially inappropriate to focus upon my *own* needs and desires. I was taught, from a very early age, that this was *wrong* and was considered to be "selfish." What I neglected to realize is that **I couldn't possibly give anything to others that I did not have myself.** I could never become *sick* enough to make others *well,* and there was no way that I could become *poor* enough to make someone else *rich!*

While I'm certainly not suggesting that anyone be selfish, I want to emphasize how beneficial it is for each one of us to appreciate and *accept* ourselves. It is an absolute *necessity* for us to l♥ve ourselves enough to fill our *own* cups in order to be able to *share* what we have with others. When I discovered my *own* personal strengths, I was able to be of much greater value to everyone else. I finally figured out that **it's impossible to pour from an empty cup!** Now that "my cup runneth over," I just l♥ve encouraging others to fill *their* cups with whatever allows them to feel good about themselves. Once they become inspired, they are eager to enlighten and support others. Would you like to see the original "Instructions for Living a ✴ Happy Life" (as if you had a choice)?

✳ Instructions

…an outline of
procedures intended to offer
optimum benefit to seekers of solutions.
Those who pay close attention to the **ROAD
MAPS** and guidelines of ✳ Life tend to realize
their goals more quickly and easily.

Instructions

for Living a  Happy Life

Welcome, Magnificent One!

We have been eagerly awaiting your arrival, as everyone here acknowledges how very special you are. You could not have come at a more opportune time, as the world is going through many dramatic and exciting changes and looks forward to your unique participation in this wonderful **Game of Life**. *You are hereby invited to claim your* **personal birthrights** *that are meant for you to enjoy for an entire lifetime:*

You were born...
to be absolutely **magnificent***;*
to be as **happy** *as you are willing to be,*
with **freedom of choice** *to use as you see fit;*
to enjoy **perfect health** *of body, mind, and spirit;*
to enjoy great **abundance** *of all things that are good;*
to be the **shining light** *of happiness for others to emulate;*
to learn only the **Truth** *and offer it to others who are seeking;*
to enjoy perfect **balance** *as you play and discover the wonders of life;*
to partake in whatever uplifts your spirits, then to **share** *it with others;*
to **l♥ve yourself** *unconditionally and, in turn,* **l♥ve others** *in the same way.*
In short...you were born to shine your light in the world and **enjoy** *abundant*
⁜Health ⁜Happiness ⁜Harmony ⁜Peace ⁜Playfulness ⁜Prosperity
⁜L♥ve ⁜Beauty and ⁜Joy.

Your primary mission in life is to discover what really delights you, then focus all of your attention upon that. This enables ✴ Life to l♥vingly offer you a perfect sense of balance, comfort, and well-being. Disregard those who do not understand life and accuse you of being "selfish." Others may not yet know that you can only be of benefit to them (and to all others) when you have learned to l♥ve and appreciate yourself. When you are happy…

- *Your relationships just blossom and grow with ease.*
- *You want everyone else to discover their own happiness.*
- *You find you are eager to share your abundance with everyone!*
- *Your health approaches perfection, so you are a burden to no one.*
- *Your energy level increases, so you can be of greater service to others.*

The most altruistic thing you can do is to engage in that which truly makes your heart sing—then acknowledge all of your blessings and bask in the positive possibilities that abound. When you do this, ✴ My Angel, you will be of extraordinary value to all life in this wondrous world. You will naturally want to share and circulate your abundance!

There is only ✴ L♥ve for you here in this ✴ Universe. It is up to you to either accept it or reject it; however, ✴ L♥ve is all there is. Please know that you actually can be, do, or have absolutely anything your heart desires. Just claim your gift of abundance, bask in the positive anticipation of receiving it, and know that it's on its way. When you go forth and seek joy, everything else falls into place perfectly. You, ✴ My Exquisite Masterpiece, are a creation in whom I am well pleased! You are a ✴ Divine Extension of Pure Perfection.

With Unconditional ✴ L♥ve and ✴ Unlimited Support,

✴ *The L♥ving Power that Created All That Is*

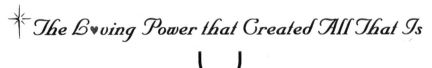

Expect a ✦ Miracle!

Dan Wakefield

If you want to
know what's really
✦**True**, just hear the voice
inside of ✦**You**!

Jacquelyn Aldana ✦ **S.o.L.**

Part 6

- Although We Are ✳ Unique, We Are All So Much the ✳ Same

- ✳ Miracle Manifestation Formula

- Amazing ✳ Miracles that Touch the ♥ Heart and Tickle the Soul

- The Magnificent ✳ Game of Life

- Can You Come Out and ✳ Play?

- 15–Minute ✳ Miracle ✳ Playshops

- 15–Minute ✳ Miracle ✳ Books

- 15–Minute ✳ Miracle ✳ Products

- Satisfaction ✳ Guarantee

We are all ✦ **ONE** on a spiritual level.

If I hurt you in some way, I also **Hurt** myself—

but as I l♥ve you, I also **L♥ve** myself!

Jacquelyn Aldana ✦ **S.o.L.**

Although We Are ✳ **Unique** We Are All So Much the **Same**

This book was written with the intention of showing you how you can easily turn large stumbling blocks into huge *stepping stones*. As you embarked upon this fascinating journey, you may have come to the same conclusions that Ron and I did, i.e., that most of us basically desire the same things in life. Typically, we want…

to l♥ve *and to* be l♥ved

to **enjoy** *a sense of* **harmony** *and* **well-being**,

to **feel free** *to pursue our dreams, and to simply* **be happy**.

As Reverend Carol Sheffield once said, "Although we may differ in skin color, religious beliefs, political preferences, occupation, gender, and culture, we are all really **ONE** on a spiritual level. Let us recognize our similarities and **celebrate our differences**, as both make up the richness of expression that fills our world." When it comes right down to it, we find that people from all parts of the globe have similar dreams and desires. As a rule, people are much more the same than they are different from one another. If you pay close attention, you'll notice that smiles and laughter are easily understood in any language. What a wonderful beginning to the creation of peace and harmony among people everywhere!

Today and every day, let's *choose* to see the best in everyone (including ourselves). Let's open our hearts and minds to "The Stream of Well-Being" and to the pure, positive energy that is always abundantly flowing toward us. We have the choice to either *accept* this magnificent energy or *reject* it. We can opt to stay *in* this life-giving stream or step *out* of it—the choice is ours. Let's now *choose* to stay *in* it and gratefully *accept* it. In fact…

Let's **choose** *to remain in* "**The Stream of Well-Being**" *from now on.*

111

✳Miracle Manifestation Formula

The hardest thing

you have to do in this life

is to **Identify** what you want,

then **Clarify** it in simple terms,

Focus all of your attention upon it,

Invite it into your life experience,

Expect you shall receive it,

then just **Accept** it

when it comes.

If you can do all of this…

You Can Have It All!

Jacquelyn Aldana ✳ S.o.L.

Amazing Miracles

that **Touch the ♥ Heart**
and **Tickle the Soul**

Marvels,

☀ Miracles, and

"Extraordinary Coincidences"

of Everyday People Who Have Applied

The 15-Minute ☀ Miracle

✴Miracles

occur naturally as

an expression

of **L♥ve**

A Course in Miracles

It Really Works!

by Alice Cabral ✦ S.o.L. of Ceres, California

I'm not exactly sure what I expected that Saturday morning when I came to
𝕿𝖍𝖊 15-𝕸inute ✦ 𝕸iracle 𝕻layshop™, but I certainly never anticipated what was about
to occur only hours later. I was so hopeful that something wonderful would happen,
yet somehow I figured it may not work for *me*. I had just gotten a new job, but it didn't
pay very much. Money was very scarce and I really needed $625 to meet my financial
obligations. I kept thinking about how good it would feel to have a little extra cash to
play with, so I wrote down that I would *appreciate* receiving unexpected income from
any and all sources (known or unknown). When I scribbled this request in my playbook,
it felt so wonderful to imagine myself enjoying life more, yet I felt a bit silly writing it
down. Little did I know I would leave the playshop, buy a lottery ticket, and win $626
the very next day (the extra $1 paid for the lottery ticket)! I immediately shouted right
out loud for the entire world to hear, "**It works! It really works!**"

It Worked Too Well!

by Larry Stone ✦ S.o.L. of Los Gatos, California

By nature I'm quite leery of things that promise wonderful outcomes with very
little effort. The only reason I attended the playshop was because my mother-in-law
enjoyed it so much that she paid for my wife and I to attend. Neither of us thought it
would make much of a difference in our lives.

We had recently started a home-based mobile mechanic business, and we just
could not seem to get it off the ground no matter what we did. Within only a few days of
applying 𝕿𝖍𝖊 15-𝕸inute ✦ 𝕸iracle, our new enterprise began to expand so fast that we
could hardly keep up with it. In fact, **we had to turn business away**! I used to always
keep my 15-𝕸inute ✦ 𝕸iracle 𝕻laybook™ in my truck, because I liked to refer to it
whenever I had a few extra minutes. Today, I decided to take it out of there, because (I
am glad to say) there's no way I can handle any more business! It sure is nice to know,
however, what to do the next time I want to attract more customers.

115

What an Experience!

by Larry LeVine ✦ S.o.L. of Mt. View, California

As a CEO of a fast-growing computer company, I have little faith in anything that sounds like a "quick fix." Nevertheless, when several of my close friends, experienced astonishing results using The 15-Minute ✦ Miracle, my curiosity got the best of me. I eagerly signed up for an entire weekend of playshops. Wow! What an experience! Before engaging in this remarkably simple process, my life consisted of working hard and wrestling with finances. Sometimes my relationships were challenging as well. In other words, life was not ideal!

The 15-Minute ✦ Miracle came into my life at just the perfect time for me. Although it provides a quick and easy way to manifest "things," I l♥ve how it inspires me to value life itself. In the moment I appreciate something (or someone), my entire world seems to expand with aliveness. I can even comfortably appreciate myself now. I feel like I have an effective tool that enables me to shift my attention from "what is" to "what I would prefer instead." Writing first thing in the morning gives me an immediate lift. It helps me to become extremely clear about my intentions and allows me to stay focused upon my objectives for the entire day.

It feels good to able to choose how I desire to feel and know in advance what I intend to accomplish. I'm so delighted when wonderful things begin to "happen" magically, with little or no effort on my part. When I don't take time to do this process, I notice that my anxiety level goes up, my energy becomes scattered, and I begin to feel off balance! Because I prefer to feel grounded, centered, and balanced, I set aside at least 15 minutes a day to do my 15-Minute ✦ Miracle. I really look forward to it.

Engaging in this process has inspired me to accept full "Response Ability" (ability to respond) for my own happiness and well-being, which allows me feel more in charge of my life. It enables me to create my preferred realities deliberately and with a sense of predictability. It has also become an invaluable tool that enables me to grow my business more easily. Because this process is so easy to use, I can see how it could benefit people anywhere in the world who want to better their lives. I only wish I had discovered it sooner!

116

The Incredible Power of Appreciation

by Gemma Bauer ✝ S.o.L. of Felton, California

For the past ten years, I have suffered from rheumatoid arthritis and have unsuccessfully tried just about every healing modality imaginable. After I first read your book, I tried to do the process the best I could. I gave up after three days, because I didn't see immediate results. It wasn't until I attended a playshop that I discovered *why* it hadn't worked for me. In my eagerness to feel better, I skipped the first step (the appreciation step). Little did I realize that a heartfelt expression of gratitude is what opens the door to attracting everything else in 𝕿𝖍𝖊 15-Minute ✝ Miracle process.

On the morning after the playshop, I did my 15-Minute ✝ Miracle with a renewed enthusiasm. This time, I made sure to first focus upon the many things that I *appreciated*. Next I wrote that I would dearly l♥ve for my body to feel 50% more flexible and comfortable. I also wanted to *do* something very special that day with my mate, Neal. In that very moment, I felt a wave of comfort and ease flooding my entire body. There was no doubt in my mind that something very wonderful was about to happen.

That day, we drove up the coast to find a special place to enjoy the day together. As we walked through the deep sand on a picturesque beach, Neal shouted at the top of his lungs, "Look, Gemma! You're moving so freely, and **you're not even limping**!" It was then that I realized how *comfortable, flexible,* and *easy* all of my movements were. **What a ✝ Miracle** to feel such tremendous freedom in my body!

My prayers were answered, and my dreams really did come true. I feel as though **my life has truly begun again**. The ease with which my body moves into each new moment now enables me to *know* that limitations are in the past. Your kind words, your l♥ving thoughts, and your extraordinary insights have deeply touched my life. Words cannot even begin to convey how very grateful I am to you and the magical 15-Minute ✝ Miracle—it has made my life worth living again. I'm sure that it's the Miracle for which I have been looking for ten long years. Thank you again for all of your love and support.

Miracle Solution for MS

by Stephanie Coffin ✝ S.o.L. of Tustin, California

When I was diagnosed with MS over a year ago, life as I knew it was over. I had almost *no* energy and suffered severe pain, spasms, and insomnia. Not only that, DMV revoked my driver's license, because I had had a seizure. I was really scared when my doctors predicted my condition would become progressively worse.

While visiting my sister, I had a chance to read the original manuscript of 𝕿𝔥𝔢 15-𝔐𝔦𝔫𝔲𝔱𝔢 ✝ 𝔐𝔦𝔯𝔞𝔠𝔩𝔢™ REVEALED that she was in the process of proofreading. As soon as I began to experiment with it, I noticed an incredible difference. For the first time in over a year, I could get through an *entire* day without several naps. I began to sleep well at night, and the pain and spasms in my body began to subside. Because I had no more seizures, I was able to get my driver's license reinstated. Within just a matter of months, **I completely overcame every symptom of MS!**

When I miss a day of doing this process, I pay for it dearly. I don't even get out of bed in the morning until I create my intentions for the day. That way, everything I do seems *easy,* my body remains *comfortable,* and my energy level stays *high.* I feel even better now than I did before I was diagnosed with multiple sclerosis. I can't even imagine going through the rest of my life without it. I want to thank you so much for giving me my life back!

All My Dreams Are Coming True

by Brooke Peterson ✝ S.o.L. of Los Gatos, California

For the first time in my life, I actually feel as though I have control over what happens to me. Before I became aware of 𝕿𝔥𝔢 15-𝔐𝔦𝔫𝔲𝔱𝔢 ✝ 𝔐𝔦𝔯𝔞𝔠𝔩𝔢, I often felt very confused and frustrated. I constantly struggled to *make* things happen. Now I enjoy total clarity with regard to my purpose in life. Whenever I get stuck, I simply turn to my 15-𝔐𝔦𝔫𝔲𝔱𝔢 ✝ 𝔐𝔦𝔯𝔞𝔠𝔩𝔢 process, and **it works every time!**

Within just three days of experimenting with this process, I manifested the perfect job that paid me abundantly and provided the freedom I needed to pursue my dreams.

Shortly after that, I reestablished my own executive placement business. Since I began sending my employees to the playshops and providing my clients with your books, my personal and professional achievements have just skyrocketed! In the last six months, I manifested over $300,000 working only part time out of my home.

I used to think I didn't have time to squeeze one more process into my busy day, but the more time I invest in my 15-Minute ✳ Miracle, the more ✳ Miracles I seem to experience. I now enjoy incredible health, more l♥ve in my life, and I feel on top of the world . The best part is that **it is all so easy**! I look forward to new discoveries and unlimited opportunities every day of my life. Each time I meet someone who feels like I *used* to, I am able to lift their spirits by sharing my remarkable ✳ Miracle stories. After all, there's nothing more inspiring than to witness a living example of prosperity and a l♥ving expression of joy.

When My House Became a Home
by Julia Stephens ✳ *S.o.L. of Los Gatos, California*

When you asked me what I really wanted that day at the Playshop, I remember saying, "I have a *house,* but what I actually want is a *home.*" You see, my husband and I were recently divorced, and I was just *existing* in "our" house. Although it provided a roof over my head, it lacked a sense of vitality and warmth, and it contained many sad memories for me. My lack of finances made it seem impossible for me to consider moving.

To my total amazement, only weeks later, my ex-husband called to tell me that he needed to buy a house for tax reasons. His *first* choice was to buy the house I was living in. I could hardly believe my ears as he tried to convince me to leave a house that I no longer wanted to stay in anyway! To make a long story short, he bought the house and gave me a generous settlement, enabling me to put a down payment on the home of my dreams. Now I not only have a beautiful *house,* but **I also have my perfect home.** I am thoroughly convinced that this serendipitous event came about as a result of doing The 15-Minute ✳ Miracle, and I plan to incorporate it into my life from now on!

Have ✴ Miracle—Will Travel!

by Debbie Voltura of San Francisco, California

For the past two years, I have struggled to find work that offered me a sense of well-being and fulfillment. One day a close friend of mine suggested that I casually experiment with 𝕿𝖍𝖊 15-𝕸inute ✴ 𝕸iracle. It was amazing—I felt better *immediately* after filling out the form! I wrote that I wanted to receive an extraordinary opportunity to express my full potential as a professional singer in a way that would ignite my passion for living. I specifically requested that it be fun and exciting, as well as financially rewarding…and I also asked that it be revealed to me ASAP.

Less than 90 minutes later the phone rang. Adrenaline flooded my veins when I realized who was calling! It was the well-known author and motivational speaker, Louise Hay. She personally invited me tour with her and provide musical inspiration for her series of **Empowering Women Seminars**. Wow! What a perfect opportunity to become abundantly prosperous while doing what I l♥ve more than anything else in the world—freely expressing my feelings through my music. 𝕿𝖍𝖊 15-𝕸inute ✴ 𝕸iracle is as valuable to me as my favorite credit card. In fact, **I don't leave home without it!**

Putting 𝕿𝖍𝖊 15-𝕸inute ✴ 𝕸iracle to the Test

by Debbie Voltura of San Francisco, California

I had *already* experienced an incredible ✴ Miracle only 90 minutes after filling out my first 15-𝕸inute ✴ 𝕸iracle form. Just in case it was only a fluke, however, I decided to really put this enigmatic process to the "test." To see what would happen, I playfully requested three things that I felt were "a bit much to ask for."

First, I requested a special *parking spot* right in front of every single place that I intended to go that day. In San Francisco, public parking spaces are all but impossible to find! Then I vividly imagined receiving some form of *unexpected income* plus some kind of *surprise gift* that would tickle my fancy. Here is an account of what actually happened all in one day:

I magically found a parking spot right in front of the first place I went that day. Although pleased, I wasn't overly impressed. When I found my perfect parking spot at the next four places, however, I became *ecstatic!* Later, I was *dumbfounded* when I opened my car door only to find a dollar bill lying in the street (the unexpected income I had playfully imagined)! As if that weren't enough, I picked up the dollar bill and almost passed out from shock—right underneath it was a beautiful, 14K-gold bracelet (obviously the surprise gift I had envisioned)! Well, I don't need any further dramatic demonstrations that The 15-Minute ✦ Miracle actually works. I now look forward to each new day, because this "Game of Life" has become much more fun to play!

Keep It Simple!

by Irene Averell ✦ S.o.L. of Sausalito, California

As a Feng Shui practitioner (offering something most people have never even heard of), I spent countless hours networking and extending complimentary consultations in order to set up my small practice. Just as it was beginning to expand, I came down with a very serious illness that took me out of commission for over a year. When I met you, things looked very bleak—lots of money going out, none coming in, and not a client in sight. I couldn't imagine how The 15-Minute ✦ Miracle could make much of a positive difference in my life.

When I asked for a magical way to attract unexpected income, I received a phone call from a reporter for a prestigious local newspaper, *The Pacific Sun*. She wanted to interview me for a small article about Feng Shui. To my amazement, she ended up writing quite an extensive article all about *my* personal practice, with my picture right on the front page! **The article yielded 65 calls,** which resulted in 52 paid consultations! These clients began referring *their* circle of friends, and I now have a glorious, growing practice.

It feels so wonderful to be back in the flow of life again. I must admit that I was reluctant to accept this idea at first, because it seemed too simple to be of any real value. I now realize that simplicity can also be extremely powerful. People who like to do things "the easy way" will really love The 15-Minute ✦ Miracle.

From Down and Out to Up 'N At 'Em

by Sunnee Kee ✝ S.o.L. of Belmont, California

About a year ago, I was extremely depressed as a result of contracting a serious illness that left me unable to work. When my boyfriend became overwhelmed with my problems and decided to leave, I was devastated. Thank God a close friend called and told me about The 15-Minute ✝ Miracle. She said, "If your life is not exactly the way you want it to be, just do this amazing little process, and watch the ✝ Miracles start to magically flow into your life." I called and ordered a book immediately! As soon as it arrived, I began doing the process right away. I specifically asked to fully regain my health, find a way to make a living doing something fun, and to become "Living Proof of Living Truth."

As of this writing, I am preparing to *play* full time working from home doing something I l♥ve that provides an abundant income. It's hard to remember how down and out I felt before, because my life is so extraordinary now. My health is perfect, my job is rewarding, and my relationship with my boyfriend has never been better. As far as I'm concerned, The 15-Minute ✝ Miracle ranks right up there with oxygen for me. It would be hard to live without it!

A Lot of Gain with No Pain

by Janette Walton of Yuma, AZ

Just shortly before I discovered The 15-Minute ✝ Miracle, I was in such physical pain and financial distress that I sometimes felt like giving up—it seemed as though things would *never* get better. I was unable to find a decent job, and the arthritis in my knees was almost unbearable. Being positive minded was difficult for me at first. I was so busy dwelling on everything that bothered me that finding the good in anything seemed impossible. Once I started to focus upon what I really *appreciated* in life, however, I began to feel a little bit better. After doing the process for about three days, I noticed that I had more energy, my body felt more flexible, and my attitude was more positive. The improvement in my health was incredible.

I am glad to report that I am now doing better than I ever have in my life! I enjoy more comfort in my body, and I see the beauty in everything. I even started my *own* business, and I'm making a lot more money and having much more fun than I ever did working for someone else. I'm certainly glad I found The 15-Minute Miracle. Every day is just full of exciting opportunities and wonderful surprises. I actually wonder how I ever got along without it!

What About Bob?

by Bob Middleton S.o.L. of Escondido, California

My life improved dramatically after attending The 15-Minute Miracle Playshop™ earlier this year. At that time, I was homeless, jobless, and extremely discouraged. Even worse, I had the social stigma of being on parole for three years. I felt totally alone in life—even my wife and family had left me.

After I began to write in My Miracle Manifestation Manual™, I was able to sleep at night without the horrible nightmares that had plagued me for years. I also noticed how much better I felt about myself and about life in general. I felt so encouraged that I began to *share* this amazing process with others on parole during my weekly group meetings. Both my doctor (who facilitated the meetings) and my parole officer were so impressed with my improved attitude that **I was officially pardoned of most of my parole**! Not only that, I now have a good job, I live with people who l♥ve me, and life seems worth living again. It feels so good to have a sense of purpose and belonging.

I now see that the way I think has *everything* to do with the way my life turns out. I really believe that everyone on preparole programs should know about this process. In fact, I now volunteer my time to teach it to those who want to learn how to make it work in their own lives. It feels good to do something that makes other people feel better about themselves. Every time I say something that offers another person a little bit of hope, I reassure myself that life can get better for me as well. By the way, if anyone tells you that dreams don't come true, you can be absolutely sure that they haven't heard about The 15-Minute Miracle!

My ✦ Miracle Money Magnet

by Heathcliff Aldana ✦ S.o.L. of Los Angeles, California

I'll always remember the first day I used the ✦ Miracle Attraction Chest™ my mom gave me as a gift. She told me to put pictures or written descriptions of things that I desired to have into the chest, and it would magically attract *more* of whatever I put into it! Although it sounded like a lot of fun, I must admit that I questioned my mother's sense of "reality" a bit.

One day on my way to work, I reached into my pocket and realized I was down to my last ten dollars. I had no idea how I was going to make it through the week on so little money. Just then, I remembered what my mom said about my little magic box. Just for fun (and feeling a bit foolish), I put the ten dollar bill into the chest. As soon as I arrived at work, I was called into my boss's office. She seemed quite upset, exclaiming, "A terrible mistake has been made!" I feared I was in some kind of trouble! To my utter amazement, she handed me a $350 check for a raise that I was supposed to have received several months earlier. I literally *ran* to the phone to call my mom to tell her what had happened! Although she was extremely pleased, she didn't seem the least bit surprised. To this day, I l♥vingly refer to my ✦ Miracle Attraction Chest™ as my magnificent "✦ Miracle Money Magnet."

A New "Leash" On Life!

by Dodie Veres ✦ S.o.L. of Los Gatos, California

One day when I was out taking a walk, a neighbor's dog (a huge Rottweiler named "Tank") decided to join me. While he was very friendly with people, he was extremely *aggressive* with other dogs. As we neared an area where several other neighborhood canines were, I began to panic as I realized that Tank may get into a serious fight. Then I really had an adrenaline rush when I discovered that he had *no collar* and that I had *no leash!* I quickly did a mental inventory of my clothing and found I had absolutely nothing I could use to improvise as a restraint device for this enormous dog.

124

Just then, I remembered 𝕿𝖍𝖊 15-𝕸𝖎𝖓𝖚𝖙𝖊 ✟ 𝕸𝖎𝖗𝖆𝖈𝖑𝖊. As I cast my eyes upward, I made my request known right out loud, "I really need a leash, and I need it right now!" To show good faith, I just kept on walking, confident that help was on the way. All of a sudden, something half-buried on the side of the road caught my eye. It was an old (but sturdy) leather belt with the buckle still intact. It was the absolutely perfect substitute for a leash *and* collar! Tank and I made it home safe and sound with no problem whatsoever—hum-m-m…what an extraordinary *coincidence* (or was it)?

Home Sweet Home

by Estie Golan ✟ S.o.L. of Campbell, California

When a good friend of mine told me about the incredible ✟ Miracles he had experienced after attending 𝕿𝖍𝖊 15-𝕸𝖎𝖓𝖚𝖙𝖊 ✟ 𝕸𝖎𝖗𝖆𝖈𝖑𝖊 𝕻𝖑𝖆𝖞𝖘𝖍𝖔𝖕™, I became eager to know more about it. Life seemed so overwhelming to me. I was drained of most of my hope and nearly all of my energy. I had been staying with friends and relatives, but had no place of my own to live—I was essentially homeless. It was extremely difficult to locate something I could afford, and most landlords were reluctant to rent to people who were self-employed. After four months of struggling to find a place to hang my hat, I was about ready to give up!

During the playshop, Jacquelyn asked me to describe my ideal living space in as much detail as possible. As I closed my eyes, I could actually see my beautiful new apartment in my mind. I even felt the warmth of the sun coming through the big picture window in the living room. As I playfully basked in my imagination, I began to gain a sense of encouragement and self-confidence. Before the day was over, I had a strong sense of positive anticipation about finding just the perfect place to live that would meet or exceed my wildest expectations.

Only six days after doing 𝕿𝖍𝖊 15-𝕸𝖎𝖓𝖚𝖙𝖊 ✟ 𝕸𝖎𝖗𝖆𝖈𝖑𝖊, I found a beautiful one-bedroom condominium with a big, sunny picture window in the living room. It's exactly what I had pictured in my mind that day at the playshop! Not only is it affordable, but it's also located very close to my office. The landlord welcomed me with open arms in spite of my self-employment status! It's all that I had imagined and much more.

What a Relief It Is!

by Chris Molinari ✝ S.o.L. of Los Gatos, California

Before I heard about 𝕿𝖍𝖊 15-𝕸𝖎𝖓𝖚𝖙𝖊 ✝ 𝕸𝖎𝖗𝖆𝖈𝖑𝖊 I was feeling incredibly stressed. I'm the founder and publisher for a magazine called *Earthworks Resource Guide* that promotes clean living and well-being for our precious earth. Although I just l♥ve my business, it is very costly to operate. My lack of adequate cash flow was causing me to panic. My constant worry about lack and limitation began to even compromise my health.

On a client's recommendation, I eagerly signed up for a weekend playshop. Because I couldn't afford to wait a month for Miracles, I arranged to get the books right away. What a relief! Any time I felt the least bit anxious or worried, I simply sat down and did my 15-𝕸𝖎𝖓𝖚𝖙𝖊 ✝ 𝕸𝖎𝖗𝖆𝖈𝖑𝖊. It was equivalent to taking a mild tranquilizer to calm my nerves and soothe my fears. Sometimes I did it a couple of times a day! Then it began to happen—one little Miracle after another. After the weekend of play-shops, the bigger Miracles began to show up. Right out the blue, a friend of mine came to visit and insisted on investing a large sum of money to promote my business (twice as much as I needed to meet all of my financial obligations). Not only that, my revenues have nearly doubled as a result of becoming clear about my desires. I plan to use this simple process to make my life a whole lot easier from now on. My new philosophy is this: If it's broke (or you're broke)…just do 𝕿𝖍𝖊 15-𝕸𝖎𝖓𝖚𝖙𝖊 ✝ 𝕸𝖎𝖗𝖆𝖈𝖑𝖊!

---

*We are allowing this space for you to share **your** personal experiences relating to your creative use of*

𝕿𝖍𝖊 15-𝕸𝖎𝖓𝖚𝖙𝖊 ✝ 𝕸𝖎𝖗𝖆𝖈𝖑𝖊

Please see page 145 and send your stories to:

♥ 𝕴𝖓𝖓𝖊𝖗 𝖂𝖎𝖘𝖉𝖔𝖒 𝕻𝖚𝖇𝖑𝖎𝖈𝖆𝖙𝖎𝖔𝖓𝖘

PO Box 1341 ✝ Los Gatos, CA 95031-1341, USA

1-(888) In The Flow*…that's (1-888-468-4335)*

The Magnificent ✳ Game of Life

For Ages: 0 and up!   **Number of Players**: Unlimited

Object of the Game: to deliberately attract and create whatever your heart desires easily and effortlessly. Since your life is actually governed by universal laws that are working *every* minute of *every* day, it is in your best interest to understand how they work. They are *absolute* and totally *impersonal,* and **no one is exempt from them.** They are always working either *for* you or *against* you —your job is to simply figure out how to invite them to work in your *favor!*

Major Universal Laws

The Law of Magnetic Attraction:

- *Like* attracts *like.*

- What you *think about* is what you *bring about!*

- What you *fill* your mind with, your life is *full* of!

The Law of Positive Expectancy:

- You'll *see* it when you *believe* it!

- All things are possible for those who *believe* that all things are possible.

- All things for which you pray and ask, *believe* that you have received them and they shall be granted you. (Mark 11:24)

The Law of Allowing:

- Accepting *others* naturally invites them to be more accepting of *you.*

- Live and *let* live as you say, "**I AM** that which **I AM**, and I agree to **ALLOW** all others to **BE** that which **THEY ARE.**" This is the *key* to feeling *free.*

- As you release *your* need to judge and control the action of others, you automatically inspire others to release *their* need to judge and control you. Oh, what a relief it is!

The Law of Cause and Effect:

- What *goes* around, *comes* around.

- For every *action,* there is an equal and opposite *reaction*.

- **YOU** are the *cause* of your life experiences. Whatever you consistently *think* about, *talk* about, and *feel*, you will eventually *experience* as a physical reality!

The Law of Gravity:

- What goes *up*, must come *down* (unless, of course, you're on the moon)!

The Law of The 15-Minute Miracle:

- What goes *down*, must come *up!* See…there's even a benefit to being down!

- If you apply the simple principles, this law has *no choice* but to work for you!

- 15 minutes per day of *focused* attention is more productive than an entire lifetime of *scattered* thinking!

Rules of The Game

- You must first *decide* what you want in life before your dreams can be realized.

- You can *receive* only as much as you *believe* you *deserve* to have!

- Anything in life is *yours* just for the asking, but first you must *ask!*

- To have at least a 95% chance of realizing your dreams, you must be *willing* to take the time to *write* down what you *desire* to experience.

- You were "born free" to *think* whatever you want to at all times! Since you can *choose* your thoughts, you can actually *choose* your destiny.

- You can make as many *choices* as you like. If at any time you become disillusioned with what you have chosen, just simply *choose* again!

- You can *be, do,* or *have* anything your heart desires, provided you are willing to… 1) Clearly *identify* it…2) *Focus* your attention upon it…3) *Expect* it with a playful sense of positive anticipation, and…4) *Accept* it when it comes!

The Facts of ✴ Life

- Whatever statement follows the words, "**I AM**" is *true* as far as ✴ Life is concerned! "**I AM**" are the two most powerful words in *any* language!

- Since you will never "get it *all* done" no matter how long you live, you might as well relax and *enjoy* the unfolding of each moment as it comes.

- You always get *second helpings* of whatever you appreciate. The "Attitude of Gratitude" *automatically* attracts things that promise to please you!

- Since you will most likely *get* whatever you *ask* for, always ask for it to come to you in just the *right time* and in ways that simply *delight* you.

- What you *resist*, persists! Whatever you *push away* or actively attempt to *get rid of,* is the very thing you will unavoidably *attract* to yourself.

- ✴ Life's favorite job is to *support* you— it *agrees* with everything you say! If you think you *can,* you're right! If you think you *can't,* you're right! No matter what you say, ✴ Life will always say, "**You're right**" and will show you why!

- ✴ Life communicates with you through your *feelings* and *emotions*. When you feel good, you are in the "flow" of life. When you feel less than good, ✴ Life is tapping you on the shoulder to tell you that you are *temporarily* out of harmony with what you *prefer*. Simply focus upon that which *thrills* and *delights* you!

- ✴ **IT** (your ✴ **Invisible Teacher**) is *always* with you! The only time ✴ **IT** *seems* to be absent is when you are negatively focused. ✴ **IT** refuses to join you in your "chain of pain." In other words, "When you *groan,* you're on your *own!*"

- There is no such thing as being a "*victim* of circumstance!" There is only "living life by *default*" when you fail to *deliberately choose* what you really *prefer* to experience. When you *know* what you *want,* you can *have* it!

- To "try" is to give yourself permission to *fail*. It actually releases any sense of responsibility to succeed. To *resolve* to do something is to invite *success*.

- *Positive* feelings yield *positive* results. The happier you are, the healthier you become. The healthier you become, the happier you are…(ad infinitum)!

✦Life's Little Idiosyncrasies

- ✦Life cannot *bring* you anything until you *ask* for it (or summon it through your *attention* to it). Heartfelt *appreciation*, vivid *imagination,* and positive *anticipation* are the best tools to use to invite desired results into your life.

- Whatever you say "Yes" to, you *automatically* invite into your life. Likewise, whatever you say "No" to, you *automatically* invite into your life! In other words, ✦Life brings you whatever you choose to *focus* your attention upon.

- ✦Life cannot hear the word *don't* when followed by the word *want.* If you say, "I *don't want* problems," ✦Life only hears, "I *want* problems!" Because ✦Life wants to bring you all that you desire, it will eagerly offer you a truckload of traumas and dramas, certain you will be enormously grateful!

✦Secrets ✦Shortcuts ✦Tips and✦Techniques

- Release and *let go* of things that no longer serve you in a positive way.

- Decide (in advance) what you would like to *be, have,* and *do* each day.

- Give yourself *permission* to be happy—do the things you l♥ve the most!

- Choose your life experiences by selectively *choosing* what you think about.

- To attract *more* of what you want, appreciate *more* of what you already have.

- Expand your horizons—instead of *observing* "what is," *envision* "what could be."

- Ask for what you want, then completely release your *attachment* to the outcome.

- The easiest way to feel good in a hurry is to find something or someone to *appreciate.*

- Your life is governed by universal laws. Make sure you *understand* how they work!

- Accept and appreciate *yourself,* so you can more easily accept and appreciate *others.*

- Embrace your *"Response Ability."* Expand your ability to respond in any situation.

- When someone pays you a compliment, be willing and ready to graciously *accept* it.

- Relieve yourself of unwanted pounds—release your need to *judge* and *control* others.

- Ask for things to come to you in just the *perfect time* in ways that totally *delight* you.

- If you're willing to settle for *less* than what you really want, that is what you'll *get!*

✳ L O V E—Language Of Vital Energy

Every thought we think and every word we speak either "adds to" or "takes away from" our sense of well-being and the well-being of others. Below are examples of ways to phrase things that can make a very positive difference in the way life unfolds for you. Every statement you *make* invites you to step into the future you *create*.

Limiting Statements	Empowering and Positive Statements
I can't believe it!	I'm so lucky. It's just the story of my life!
I just can't ...	Up until now, I couldn't…
I don't want to…	I prefer to…
I don't want to be late.	I prefer to be at least ten minutes early.
Don't forget to…	Remember to…
I'll *try* to...	I intend to find the perfect way to…
Don't…	It's best to....
You made me feel…	When you _____, I felt _____.
I want to get rid of…	I look forward to…
I hate getting up in the morning.	I l♥ve to leap out of bed every morning with a sense of positive anticipation and unstoppable enthusiasm.
Watch out! That's dangerous! Be careful! You could get hurt!	It feels so good to remember that **FEAR** is just an acronym for **F**orgetting **E**verything's **A**ll **R**ight!
Life is hard—it's just the story of my life!	No matter what I do or how I do it, things just seem to work out perfectly for me—it's just the story of my life!

The Quickest Way to Diffuse an Argument
...is to just calmly say these four simple words:

"You may be right!"

Words to WIN by...

- *Expect* a ✷ Miracle!—*Dan Wakefield*

- What you *want*, wants *you!*—*Debra Jones*

- If you can *dream* it, you can *do* it!—*Walt Disney*

- Miracles happen—why not to *you?*—*Ron Aldana*

- If you don't *ask*, you don't *get!*—*Mahatma Gandhi*

- If you *know* what you *want*, you can *have* it!—*RHJ*

- Dare to dream the "*I'm Possible*" dream!—*Jacquelyn Aldana*

- Dreams are *Miracles* just waiting to happen!—*Jacquelyn Aldana*

- Your dreams are *previews* of coming attractions!—*Denis Waitley*

- I've been rich, and I've been poor...and *rich* is better!—*Mae West*

- What you *think about* is what you *bring about!*—*Jacquelyn Aldana*

- Whether you think you *can* or you *can't,* you're *right!*—*Henry Ford*

- The more you *have*, the more you have to *give!*—*Jacquelyn Aldana*

- What you *fill* your mind with, your life is *full* of!—*Dr. Richard Green*

- *Laughter* is the shortest distance between two people!—*Victor Borge*

- If you want to *Real-ize* it, just simply ✷ *Miracle-ize* it!—*Heathcliff Aldana*

- Miracles occur *naturally* as an expression of l♥ve.—*A Course in Miracles*

- Either *nothing* is a ✷ Miracle, or *everything* is a ✷ Miracle!—*Albert Einstein*

- Luck is what happens when *preparation* meets *opportunity!*—*H. Jackson Brown, Jr.*

- When you take *responsibility* for your life, your *"Response Ability"* soars.—*Larry LeVine*

Note: When you understand The Major Universal Laws and apply the quick and simple principles of 𝕿𝖍𝖊 15-𝕸𝖎𝖓𝖚𝖙𝖊 ✷ 𝕸𝖎𝖗𝖆𝖈𝖑𝖊, you will discover, for yourself, just how magical life can be for you every day from this day forward. Congratulations! From now on, you can play this **Magnificent ✷ Game of Life** and expect to **WIN!**

Can You
Come Out
and  Play?

At least six times a year, we offer a variety of playshops at our ranch in the Santa Cruz Mountains (located in the central coast region of California) where the air smells exceptionally fresh and clean. The mountain views are absolutely beautiful, and the energy surrounding the **SUMMIT SUNRISE RANCH** seems almost *magical* among the oaks and redwoods that are indigenous to that area.

People come from near and far to renew their spirits and discover an amazingly simple way to **fall in l♥ve**—in l♥ve with Life and everything in it, (including themselves)! People literally **ignite with delight** when they begin to realize all of the wonderful possibilities that are available to them! When you make the conscious connection between "what you think" and "what you experience," you can deliberately choose your life experiences. Once you discover how you *unintentionally* attract unwanted circumstances into your life, you can then *deliberately* attract that which you *prefer* instead. This awareness enables you to take your rightful place in the driver's seat of life! If you prefer "foresight" to "hindsight," you'll be very glad you came.

If you are inspired to participate in any of our activities, just call us **Toll Free** at **1-(888) In The Flow** (that's 1-888-468-4335) to make the necessary arrangements. Because our gatherings are very experiential, we usually keep our groups relatively small (12 to 14 participants). For that reason, you may want to reserve your space well in advance. Life offers us unlimited potential, and there are multitudes of Miracles just waiting for you to call them forth.

Level I—The *✴S.o.L. Certification Program

This life-enhancing foundation course often serves as "the missing piece to the puzzle of life." It empowers you to easily get to where you want to go very quickly. You can expect to actually *master* the magical 15-Minute✴Miracle process in a single day, which will inspire and uplift you for the rest of your life! The best part is that it is all so simple, yet so incredibly powerful. This exhilarating course takes you from "wishing and hoping" to "believing and knowing" that **you can have it all!** If you're looking for a **ROAD MAP to ✴Miracles,** look no further. We'll share several shortcuts to success that have proven to work for countless others just like you. When you focus upon the fulfillment of your desires, **your dreams have no choice but to come true!**

Level II—The **✴F.U.N. Certification Program

If you liked **Level I,** you'll l♥ve **Level II,** because it tends to take you from the launching pad to "**lift off**!" It reveals intriguing secrets that make the difference between "just existing" and "really living." You will learn how to cause the doors of opportunity and the floodgates of abundance to fly wide open for you! You will quickly be able to clarify what makes your heart sing with regard to your life and your livelihood. In short, you will learn how to *deliberately* attract and create whatever you truly desire in life more easily and effortlessly than ever before! This playful (yet empowering) course will very likely take you beyond where you have ever been before in terms of conscious awareness and deliberate creation. **Level II** invites you to say "yes" and "know!" Say "yes" to ✴Life and "know" that all things *are* really possible!

*✴S.o.L. = **S**tudent **o**f **L**ife (or **S**ender **o**f **L**♥ve, **S**pirit **o**f **L**ight, **S**o **O**bviously **L**ucky)
✴F.U.N. = **Free and **U**nlimited **N**ow!

THE "Get A Round Tuit 'N Do It" PLAYSHOP™

How to Easily Transform **Procrastination** into ✳**Accomplishment**!

Is there something in your life that you want to do (or think you *should* do), but somehow it's just not getting done? On the days you finally decide to *force* yourself to tackle a project (one you have great *resistance* to even starting), do you find yourself having to get something to eat, go to the bathroom, get something to drink, go to the bathroom again, make several phone calls, watch something (anything) on TV, then take a nap? Do you honestly accomplish very much...or do you just feel frustrated, exhausted, and guilty at the end of the day? If any of this sounds familiar, you'll be glad to know that now there is a fun, easy, and enjoyable way to accomplish whatever you would like to do, in a way that leaves you feeling very good about yourself! Learn an easy, step-by-step process that makes any task seem fun and "do-able."

This solution-oriented playshop reveals the key to success when it comes to creating a sense of order in your life. It is cleverly designed to provide a delightful and entertaining way for you to easily accomplish goals of any magnitude. No longer will you be confined to living in "The Valley of Hopeless Overwhelm." If you are tired of feeling guilty about always "putting things off," you will be thrilled to discover that there's a fun and easy way to start (and finish) your projects. This unique and interesting technique is amazingly *simple,* extremely *creative,* and enormously *rewarding.* Many people claim they are achieving, in only a few days, things that used to take them weeks (even months) to accomplish. This program is designed to be done with a partner, so find a friend who wants to *play,* and sign up for this engaging...

*"Go-With-the-***Flow***, Make-Your-Life-***Easier***,
and Have-***Fun***-Getting-Organized Playshop."*

It promises to "lighten your load and light up your life!"

The  Elite Retreat

If you are ready to cleanse your body, clear your mind, and claim your spirit, you will really appreciate this **2 ½-day MINI VACATION.** It's ideal if you want to create a brand new and wonderful life for yourself. It promises to leave you feeling totally *refreshed, renewed,* and *reborn!* All food and lodging are included in price of tuition.

1) **Cleanse Your Body**: You will be l♥vingly pampered and served tasty, life-giving organically-grown food that allows your body to rest and renew itself. It's a great way to say "thanks" to your body for taking such good care of you.

2) **Clear Your Mind**: You will have the perfect opportunity to wipe your slate clean as you release and let go of anything in your life that no longer serves you in a positive way. This creates infinite space for new and better things with which to fill your mind. Ah-h-h-h—a fresh, new beginning!

3) **Claim Your Spirit**: Now you can easily top off your life with abundant l♥ve, light, and laughter. You are invited to completely rewrite "The Story of Your Life." This is your chance to reunite with who you truly are. So go ahead—give yourself permission to dream The "I'm possible Dream" and take giant steps forward toward becoming the best you can be! Create the "New You," and become your own "Best Friend!"

NOTE: All books, materials, gifts, and certificates are included in the price of each playshop. **Just bring your desire to be happy—everything else is provided!** Feel free to call for a current schedule of events and rate information. If you would like to sponsor a 15-Minute ✳ Miracle Playshop™ or Seminar in *your* geographic area, please feel free to call us **TOLL FREE at 1-888-468-4335** to make the necessary arrangements. We look most forward to hearing from you.

The 15-Minute ✳ Miracle™ REVEALED

You'll love this life-enhancing book, because it was written **all about you**! It definitely has the potential to lift your spirits from the "depths of despair" to the "heights of delight" in an amazingly short period of time. Once you experiment with the simple 15-Minute ✳ Miracle process, your well-being will begin to soar. In fact, you'll wonder how you ever got along without it! It empowers you to deliberately attract whatever your heart desires with incredible ease. You will also discover how to feel good *no matter what* your personal challenges may be. This feel-good book is one of the many items that are part of the ✳ Miracle Attraction Chest™. It is also included in the price of the tuition for the **Level I** 15-Minute ✳ Miracle Playshop™.   **$16.95**

My ✳ Miracle Manifestation Manual™

This book will *supercharge* your life! It's your own **Personal ✳ Miracle Journal**, complete with a 31-day supply of My 15-Minute ✳ Miracle forms. It's loaded with lots of great examples to inspire and motivate you to create ✳ Miracles of your own. It allows you to magically attract wonderful things. By investing just 15 minutes a day to express your desires in writing, you will experience positive life changes that will very likely astound you! You will wonder how anything so *easy* could actually be so *powerful*. This book is included the "**Miracle Starter Kit**" *(see page 146)* and in both versions of the ✳ Miracle Attraction Chest™ as well as the **Level I** 15-Minute ✳ Miracle Playshop™ **$12.95**

Everything You Ever Wanted to Know About
The 15-Minute ✳ Miracle™

This little book was written to explain exactly what The 15-Minute ✳ Miracle is and how it has been successfully used to create more joy in people's lives. It consists of

36 of the most frequently asked questions. The answers explain how it was created, what the *benefits* are, and what you can expect it to do for *you*. It's ideal to share with your friends, because it offers lots of examples of how people have used it to *regain* their balance, *clarify* their desires, and *attract* ✴ Miracles. It features several true stories of people who have discovered how to quickly "jumpstart" their lives with it. It's part of the **Level I Playshop** and both versions of the ✴ Miracle Attraction Chest. $4.95

The 15-Minute ✴ Miracle™ (Work) Playbook™

This entertaining playbook enables you to have fun while greatly expanding your use of The 15-Minute ✴ Miracle process. It's not merely a book to *read,* but rather a book to *do!* By simply engaging in the solution-oriented exercises, you can readily learn to attract whatever your heart desires more quickly and easily then every before. In this book, we pose thought-provoking questions for you to consider. As you explore your thoughts and feelings, you will experience more harmony in your relationships, greater acceptance of yourself, and more ease and joy in your life. This playfully written workbook is also included in your tuition for **The ✴ Elite Retreat**. $24.95

Get A Round Tuit 'N Do It
How to Easily Transform **Procrastination** into ✴ **Accomplishment**!

This uniquely-written book is a creative power tool that offers you enormous encouragement, and it *automatically* enables you to **get organized and get things done with incredible ease**. It clearly shows you (in a way that is actually enjoyable), how you can quickly *accomplish* things that tend to overwhelm you. People are claiming to get more done in one day than they were previously accomplishing in weeks. In fact, many people say they are finishing projects that they could not even bring themselves to start, prior to doing this process! It's extremely *easy* and a lot of *fun!* Because it works best when you have a partner, you may want to get an extra book. When you order two at a time, you receive a 20% discount on both books. This "fun-to-do" workbook is included in The **Get A Round Tuit 'N Do It** Playshop™. $15.95

✳ Miracle Attraction Chest™

This item is sometimes compared to the intriguing **Aladdin's Lamp** (except it's not limited to only *three* wishes). It includes four inspiring books: this book, plus *My ✳ Miracle Manifestation Manual™*, *✳ Secrets ✳ Solutions & ✳ Shortcuts to Miracles*, and *Everything You Ever Wanted to Know About The 15-Minute ✳ Miracle™*. It also includes a spectacular array of quality *gifts* that promote a wonderful sense of well-being and positive expectancy. It's the perfect place to keep pictures and descriptions of those things you really want to magically attract into your life with amazing ease.

It works extremely well, because it encourages us to make our desires very *clear* by writing them down or finding pictures of that which we desire to attract. Then we can just drop them into our little magic box and *forget* about them. The energy of our thoughts begins to pulse and attract the physical equivalent of that which we have focused our attention upon. Please read the humorous story entitled "**My ✳ Miracle Money Magnet**" on page 124 of this book for an inspiring example. This unique gift is absolutely perfect for "The Person Who **Doesn't** Have Everything!" It includes over $60 worth of books, gifts, and delightful surprises.   **$49.95**

The ✳ Luxury Edition is a beautiful, hand-crafted mahogany chest featuring a collector's quality rosewood pen set. Antique brass hinges and trim accent the richly-finished wood, making this ✳ *Deluxe Miracle Attraction Chest™* one of the most exquisite gifts you could ever give to someone. Designed in the form of an antique book, it complements the finest furniture and accessories. It includes additional reading material and a variety of intriguing gifts that promise to warm the heart, uplift the soul, and inspire the creation of ✳ Miracles. Whoever receives it from you will cherish it and keep it forever! We will be glad to gift wrap it for you and ship it anywhere in the world.   **$149.95**

Satisfaction ✦ Guarantee

I, _____, hereby promise to set aside a full fifteen (15) minutes each day to fill out My 15-Minute ✦ Miracle forms for the next three weeks! The key to my success is in taking this time to deliberately focus all of my attention upon my dreams and desires (daydreaming is highly encouraged). Starting today, I truly expect to realize more enjoyment and satisfaction in my life as a result of applying the simple (yet powerful) 15-Minute ✦ Miracle principles.

Should I not experience a greater sense of well-being after consistently doing My 15-Minute ✦ Miracle process for a period of twenty-one (21) consecutive days, then ♥ Inner Wisdom Publications agrees that I am entitled to a full refund of my tuition fee, (less materials) with no questions asked. In other words, I am guaranteed either a happier and more fulfilling life or a refund of my investment!

Either way, I win!

Inner Wisdom Publications
_____
♥ Inner Wisdom Publications

_____
Signature of Participant

Date _____

140

Bibliography
Inspirational Food for Thought

Author	Name of Book	Publisher
Jacquelyn Aldana	The 15-Minute Miracle™ REVEALED	♥ *Inner Wisdom Pub.*
Jacquelyn Aldana	The 15-Minute Miracle (No Work) Playbook™	♥ *Inner Wisdom Pub.*
Jacquelyn Aldana	My Miracle Manifestation Manual™	♥ *Inner Wisdom Pub.*
Jacquelyn Aldana	Get A Round Tuit 'N Do It™	♥ *Inner Wisdom Pub.*
Marcus Bach	The World of Serendipity	*Prentice-Hall*
Richard Bach	Jonathan Livingston Seagull	*Avon*
Richard Bach	Illusions	*Dell*
Ken Blanchard*	The One-Minute Manager	*Burke*
J. Allen Boone	Kinship With All Life	*Harper & Row*
Joan Brady	God on a Harley	*Pocket Books*
Claude M. Bristol*	The Magic of Believing	*Cornerstone Library*
David D. Burns, M.D.	Feeling Good—The New Mood Therapy	*A Signet Book*
Dr. Leo Buscaglia*	Living, Loving, and Learning	*Ballantine Books*
Canfield & Hansen*	The Aladdin Factor	*Berkeley Books*
Canfield & Hansen*	Chicken Soup for the Soul	*Health Comm. Inc.*
Dr. Deepak Chopra*	Quantum Healing	*Bantam*
Alan Cohen*	The Dragon Doesn't Live Here Anymore	*Alan Cohen Pub.*
Lee Coit*	Listening	*Las Brisas Retreat*
Norman Cousins	Anatomy of an Illness	*Bantam*
Stephen R. Covey*	7 Habits of Highly Effective People	*Simon and Schuster*
Dr. Wayne W. Dyer*	Real Magic	*Harper*
Dr. Wayne W. Dyer*	You'll See It When You Believe It	*Harper*
Ralph Waldo Emerson	Emerson's Essays	*Thomas Crowell Co.*
Fisher & Robbins	Tranquillity Without Pills	*Bantam*
Jean K. Foster	The God-Mind Connection	*Walsworth Pub.*
Foundation for Inner Peace*	A Course in Miracles	*Found. Inner Peace*
M. Goulston/P. Goldberg	Get Out of Your Own Way	*Perigee Books*
Louise L. Hay*	You Can Heal Your Life	*Hay House, Inc.*
Jerry & Esther Hicks*	A New Beginning II	*Crown Intern'l*

Author	Name of Book	Publisher
Jerry & Esther Hicks*	Sara and the Foreverness of Friends of a Feather	*Abraham-Hicks*
Napoleon Hill*	Think and Grow Rich	*Ballantine Books*
Napoleon Hill*	Law of Success	*Success Unlimited*
Debra Jones*	What You Want, Wants You	*Health Comm., Inc.*
Jon Kabat-Zinn*	Wherever You Go There You Are	*Hyperion*
Philip P. Kavanaugh, M.D.	Magnificent Addiction	*Aslan Publishing*
Barbara Ann Kipfer	14,000 Things to Be Happy About	*Workman Pub.*
Dr. Leonard Laskow	Healing With Love	*Harper-San Fran.*
Barbara Hoberman Levine	Your Body Believes Every Word You Say	*Aslan Publishing*
Allan P. Lewis	Clearing Your Life Path	*Homana Publishing*
Maxwell Maltz, M.D.	Psycho-Cybernetics	*Pocket Books of NY*
Og Mandino*	The Greatest Secret In The World	*Frederick Fell, Inc.*
Eugene Maurey	The Power of Thought	*Midwest Books*
Peter McWilliams*	You Can't Afford the Luxury of a Negative Thought	*Prelude Press*
Marlo Morgan	Mutant Message Down Under	*Harper-Collins*
Arnold M. Patent*	You Can Have It All	*Beyond Words Pub.*
Norman Vincent Peale*	The Power of Positive Thinking	*Fawcett-Crest*
Norman Vincent Peale*	You Can If You Think You Can	*Spire Books*
Paul Pearsall, Ph.D.	Making Miracles	*Prentice Hall Press*
Catherine Ponder	Dare to Proper!	*Devorss & Company*
James Redfield*	The Celestine Prophecy	*Warner Books, Inc.*
RHJ (anonymous author)	It Works	*DeVorss & Co.*
David J. Schwartz	The Magic of Thinking Big	*Wilshire Book Co.*
Florence Scovel Shinn	The Game of Life and How to Play It	*DeVorss & Co.*
Dr. Bernie S. Siegel*	Love, Medicine, & Miracles	*Harper & Row*
Jose Silva & Robert Stone*	You The Healer	*Instant Improvement*
Robert Skutch	Journey Without Distance	*Celestial Arts*
Doreen Virtue, Ph.D.*	I'd Change My Life If I Had the Time	*Hay House, Inc.*
Dan Wakefield	Expect A Miracle	*Harper-Sam Fran.*
Neale Donald Walsch*	Conversations With God—Book 1	*G.P. Putnam's Sons*
Neale Donald Walsch*	Conversations With God—Book 2	*Hampton Roads*
Mary Ann Williamson*	Return to Love	*Harper-Collins*
Oprah Winfrey/Bob Greene	Make the Connection	*Hyperion*

*To the best of my knowledge, these authors have audio and/or videotapes available
at this time. You may obtain them from your local bookseller or contact their publishers directly.

⸙ Index